DESTINY

THE OFFICIAL COOKBOOK

DESTINY ®

THE OFFICIAL COOKBOOK

BY VICTORIA ROSENTHAL

INSIGHT
EDITIONS

San Rafael · Los Angeles · London

CONTENTS

INTRODUCTION

I was enjoying a lovely afternoon tea with my good friend Tess Everis when she implored me to give her my sandwich recipe. Though I was happy to oblige, I realized that my favorite drinks, meals, and desserts were scattered among my notes, my messy kitchen, and obscure corners of my own memory. I was embarrassed to admit that my recipes weren't easily accessible, but Tess came up with a great solution, suggesting that I put together a collection of all my favorite recipes. "We can't rely on you to bake for everyone every time the Dawning comes around!" she said.

I haven't always been in charge of all the holidays and cultural touchstones in the Last City. You may have come across my shop at some point, where I sold beautiful fabrics and armor patterns. For a long time, I was content with putting together new color themes on occasion and seeing the smiles on people's faces as they tried out new attire. My first opportunity to plan holiday events came when I hosted the inaugural Festival of the Lost at the Tower, during which I was able to do a little organizing and see what I could do to bring the community together.

And then the Red War happened, and I found myself on a battlefield. Instead of handing out shaders, I was coordinating scouting missions. I witnessed the Guardians lose their Light first-hand, and I saw the light in the eyes of those whom they protected dim. But we didn't give up, and against all odds we escaped with our lives and retook our beautiful city from the Cabal. I had to spend some time recovering from serious injuries, and I'll never forget what it was like to see my friends lose hope.

Which brings me back to my friend Tess. I don't know if I would have returned to the Last City if it weren't for her teasing me about what I was missing. I was shocked when she told me they had looked through my terminal and were setting up holidays without my input. It took me some time to realize how much my holidays meant to others. I took to heart my lessons from the Red War of the importance of morale and saw an opportunity. I petitioned the Vanguard for help with some new celebrations I wanted to host, and the rest is history.

To come up with these new events, I chatted with some very familiar faces in the Last City and even borrowed a few ideas from friends. But most importantly, I pored over some Golden Age engrams, discovering delicious foods from the past that I can't wait to share with everyone. We've been so busy worrying about surviving all the dangers of the present day that we've forgotten the joys we used to share. Old Eva can't host a party every day, but this collection of recipes can make any day a little more special. And if I can bring even a small spark to your life, then I'll have done what I could to help.

—Eva Levante

MEALS IN THE LAST CITY

Humanity is strongest when we work together. The Tower only exists as the last beacon of hope because of the many people who put their hearts and souls into keeping it safe. I'm not just talking about the Guardians, either. All the people here and abroad toil every day to keep the dream of a better tomorrow alive. I love using food and drink to bring people together, so I thought there was no better way to help unite us all than to assemble this cookbook. Although the Guardians certainly have a unique set of needs, we all need something in our bellies to feel full and satisfied.

It's thanks to the strongest personalities in the Tower that I was inspired to come up with so many unique recipes, so I wanted to include a set meal that best represents each of them and includes their favorite dishes. Commander Zavala tries to uphold a cold exterior, but his care for all who live in the Tower is apparent by how hard he fights to keep everyone safe. Amanda Holliday is a clever shipwright who works tirelessly. Both of them take the time to enjoy a hearty meal that keeps their energy up. Ikora Rey is as stoic as she is strong-willed, but she can put that aside when enjoying her favorite extravagantly spiced dishes. It hurts to think about Cayde-6, but his passion for adventuring and gambling was trumped only by his love of ramen. Suraya Hawthorne has found her calling of keeping the clans organized and motivated, but her new life in the City can't temper her love for eating on the go. Anastasia Bray might spend too much time thinking about the past, but her love of Camrin Dumuzi brings her to the present where perhaps the two can pause to enjoy a fine dinner. And I may not like spending time with the Drifter, but he'll always make time for a good meal.

IKORA REY AND OSIRIS

- Kefta
- Gambas al Ajillo
- Lamb Tagine
- Roasted Vegetable Couscous Salad
- Invective

AMANDA HOLLIDAY AND ZAVALA

- Hush Puppies
- Buttermilk Biscuits
- Fried Chicken
- Coleslaw
- Sunshot

CAYDE-6

- Gyoza
- Spicy Ramen
- Gyudon
- Ajitsuke Tamago
- Ace of Spades

DEVRIM KAY AND SURAYA HAWTHORNE

- Eliksni Birdseed
- Beef Jerky
- Split Pea Soup
- Tomato and Roasted Garlic Focaccia
- S'mores Bark

ANA BRAY AND CAMRIN DUMUZI

- Spinach Salad
- Rack of Lamb
- Herb Potato Stacks
- White Chocolate Travelers
- The Vow

THE DRIFTER

- Duck Poutine
- Banh Mi Burgers
- Elotes
- Thorn
- Dark Chocolate Motes

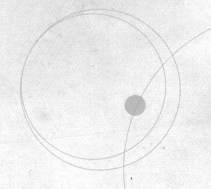

ENTERTAINING

One of my favorite things to do is invite all my friends over for dinner parties. Nothing makes a party like a table covered in everyone's favorite foods. If you feel nervous about taking that on, I hope this cookbook is your window to more confidence in the kitchen. Look through the recipes and start with the easier dishes before working your way up to something more complicated. And if you get stuck, there are always the drink recipes, which are even simpler!

This shouldn't be a surprise if you are a Guardian, but non-Guardians shouldn't feel odd about inviting their friends with Ghosts over for a meal. A person's life is quite different if they return as a Guardian, but they still need to eat to keep themselves alive. A Ghost may be able to bring their partner back from the dead, but experiencing starvation is not worth skipping out on a few meals. I can barely function by the end of the day if I miss lunch!

If you are looking for an excuse to have a large group of friends over, this cookbook covers many meal ideas for the holidays. During the Crimson Days, show those you love how much you appreciate them with a delicious feast. The Revelry is a time to recharge and enjoy finger foods in between adventures in the Verdant Forest, and the Festival of the Lost commemorates those who've left us behind by wishing them safe travels in the next life. The Dawning is perfect for surprising your friends with gifts and delights. I could go on and on about decoration ideas for each holiday, but Tess told me that if I don't focus on food, this book will require an engram to view. Perhaps I'll compile a list of holiday traditions in the future.

INGREDIENTS GUIDE

Throughout my years of creating recipes, I have found joy in researching so many unique ingredients and kitchen techniques. The library holds countless records of the Golden Age: all the different ingredients and how to combine them, as well as suggestions for replacements when items were scarce. Oh, how exciting it would have been to be a Golden Age chef. Since the Collapse occurred, it's become more difficult to find the same variety of ingredients, so I have had to learn to be conscious of what I can find and plan around these limitations. I will enjoy passing what I've learned along to you, my friend.

I know some of you reading this collection of recipes are just starting out in the kitchen, so I want to explain some of the more unusual ingredients we'll be using. Understanding your ingredients and how to use them will help you build up your culinary skills. You'll notice I'm partial to cuisines originating from various corners of pre-Collapse Earth; many of these items may be tucked away in less obvious corners of the City and marked up for a fair bit of Glimmer, and some may require a postmaster to ship and deliver them to you.

ANCHO CHILE is a dried poblano pepper. It has a Scoville scale rating between 1,000 and 1,500 SHU. This can be replaced with another dried chile of your choice with a similar heat level, but keep in mind that the flavor will be slightly different. Ancho chiles can be stored in a cool pantry.

BONITO FLAKES, also known as katsuobushi, are dried tuna shavings. They are a key ingredient in Japanese cuisine and are one of the major components in dashi. Bonito flakes can be used to enhance the flavors of stocks and used as a garnish. They can be stored in a cool pantry.

CREMA MEXICANA is a creamy and mildly sour condiment. It is slightly thicker than heavy cream. This item can be substituted with its French equivalent, crème fraîche, or heavy cream, with a teaspoon of lemon juice for every cup. Crema Mexicana should be stored in a refrigerator.

DASHI STOCK is a basic fish stock used in Japanese cuisine. It is made by combining kombu and bonito flakes with water. Dashi stock must be stored in the refrigerator once cooked and can be kept up to five days.

DIASTATIC MALT POWDER is a grain that has been sprouted, dried, and then ground into a powder. It contains active enzymes that release sugars and will help yeast grow. Adding it when baking will help improve the rise of the dough and help the crust become golden.

EUROPEAN-STYLE BUTTER is traditionally churned longer than typical butter and will have higher butterfat percentage (about 82 percent). The higher butterfat count results in a butter with a softer texture and quicker melt time. You can certainly use regular butter if you don't have access, but European-style butter does make a difference!

GOCHUJANG is a thick Korean chili paste that contains red chili peppers, sticky rice, fermented soybeans, and sweeteners. Heat levels of gochujang can vary and are typically displayed on the container with a spice indicator. Once gochujang is opened, it must be stored in an airtight container in the refrigerator.

KIMCHI is a spicy fermented vegetable dish popular in Korean cuisine. Napa cabbage is the most common vegetable used for kimchi. It is prepared with brine and spices, similar to a pickling process. Kimchi goes beyond that and allows the vegetables to ferment. Kimchi must be stored in the refrigerator.

KOMBU is a type of dried kelp used in Japanese cuisine to enhance the flavors of stocks. It can be stored in a cool pantry.

KOREAN PEAR, which is sometimes also labeled as Asian pear, is a large pear with brown speckled skin grown in Asia. Korean pears are used in Korean barbecue marinades for their sweetness and their help in tenderizing meat. If Korean pears are difficult to find, they can be substituted with kiwis for tenderizing purposes. Bosc pears can also be used as a similar taste, but they don't tenderize meat the same way. Korean pears can be stored at room temperature for about a week or in a refrigerator for several months.

MISO is a paste made of fermented soybeans used in Japanese cuisine. Miso comes in several varieties including white (the mildest flavor) and red (allowed to age longer, making it saltier with a stronger flavor). Miso can be stored in an airtight container in the refrigerator.

NORI is a dried edible sheet of seaweed used in Japanese cuisine. It is most popularly used for wrapping sushi rolls. Nori can be stored in a cool pantry.

QUESO ASADERO is a mild, semisoft cheese used in Mexican cuisine. It has a very similar texture to string cheese and is used as a melting cheese. If queso asadero is difficult to find, it can be substituted with Monterey Jack or Muenster cheese. Queso asadero can be stored in the refrigerator.

QUESO COTIJA is a hard, crumbly cheese used in Mexican cuisine. The cheese is traditionally aged, which gives it its salty flavor. If queso cotija is difficult to find, it can be substituted with feta cheese. Queso cotija can be stored in the refrigerator.

QUESO FRESCO is a fresh, soft Mexican cheese made from cow's milk. The cheese has a salty and very mild flavor. It can be substituted with a mild feta cheese. Queso fresco should be stored in the refrigerator.

SAMBAL OELEK is a ground chili paste used in South Asian cuisine. The chili peppers are combined with garlic and ginger. If sambal oelek is difficult to find, it can be substituted with another hot sauce. Sambal oelek must be stored in the refrigerator once opened.

SICHUAN PEPPERCORNS are a reddish spice, similar in size to black pepper, grown in China. These peppercorns give your mouth a unique numbing sensation. Sichuan peppercorns can be stored in a pantry.

SHICHIMI TOGARASHI is a seven-flavor chili spice mix used in Japanese cuisine. I have included a recipe to make your own homemade version. Shichimi togarashi can be stored in a pantry.

TOMATILLO is a tart fruit wrapped in a papery husk that is grown in Mexico. It should not be confused with a green tomato. Tomatillos, with the husk still on, can be stored in the refrigerator for about two weeks.

DIETARY CONSIDERATIONS

There are ingredients in this cookbook that may conflict with your dietary restrictions. Don't feel limited by the recipes: Experiment, substitute when needed, and always try to improve yourself in the kitchen! If Amanda Holliday can learn to make something without burning her kitchen down, you should be just fine. And if you happen to be a Guardian, maybe your Ghost can shed some light as well.

ADAPTING TO VEGETARIAN DIETS

Several recipes in this book are vegetarian friendly. Many other recipes can be adapted to your dietary needs. Replace meat broths with vegetable broths. Swap out proteins with your favorite grilled vegetable or meat substitute. This will affect the cooking times, so plan ahead.

ADAPTING TO GLUTEN-FREE DIETS

For most recipes, you can use equal ratios of gluten substitute for flour, but be prepared to modify the quantity just in case the consistency seems off.

ADAPTING TO LACTOSE-FREE DIETS

Feel free to replace milk and heavy cream with your favorite nondairy milk. There are also plenty of butter alternatives that I would highly recommend using to replace butter in recipes. I don't normally suggest replacing butter with oil because it doesn't hold together as well. If you do try it, approach it in smaller batches.

BASICS

Although my days of outfitting Guardians are behind me, I've learned quite a few things over the years about bringing people joy. Every good outfit needs a strong foundation. Sometimes it's that perfect contrast of colors or original pattern work that really tells the world you've arrived.

In the same way, if I'm going to be sharing cheer with delicious treats and dishes, I have to start with a strong base. I've included a few essential recipes to help any good cook get started, and the best part about them is that you can use them on all sorts of dishes. Although I'll be including these basic elements in many of the recipes throughout this book, you should feel free to experiment with them in new and creative ways. But if you find yourself in a fix even your trusty Ghost can't help you out of, don't be afraid to ask for help. It takes a stronger person to admit you're in over your head than it does to fail alone!

LEMON GARLIC PEPPER SALT

Lemons can be so difficult to find around the Tower. Whenever a merchant has some, I buy as many as I can carry. By using several of them for the zest in this recipe, I have access to that lovely lemon flavor all year round. And don't forget to include the citric acid if you can obtain it, as it really makes everything pop.

- 🛡 **Difficulty: Easy**
- 🕐 **Prep time: 30 minutes**
- 🔥 **Cook time: 1 hour**
- ⚠ **Yield: ½ cup**
- 🏔 **Used in: Chicken Broth** (page 25), **Avgolemono** (page 41), **Hush Puppies** (page 53), **Smoked Turkey Legs** (page 107)

8 lemons, zested
3 tablespoons black peppercorns
1 tablespoon dried oregano
¼ cup garlic powder
2 tablespoons salt
2 teaspoons citric acid (optional)

1. Preheat oven to 170°F. Mix the lemon zest and peppercorns together on a baking sheet. Place in the oven for 35 minutes, or until the lemon is dry but not burnt.

2. Remove from the oven and allow to cool. Transfer to a spice grinder, and grind the peppercorns for 10 to 20 seconds. The ingredients should be well ground but not as fine as a powder. Place in a bowl, and combine with the dried oregano, garlic powder, salt, and citric acid, if using. Place in an airtight container, and store for up to 4 months.

SPICY SMOKED PAPRIKA SALT

This spice combination is the perfect thing to bring with you for those long treks outside of the Tower and is an excellent savory addition to any dish that can enhance even the drabbest rations.

- 🛡 **Difficulty: Easy**
- 🕐 **Prep time: 5 minutes**
- ⚠ **Yield: ½ cup**
- 🏔 **Used in: Kefta** (page 31), **Gambas al Ajillo** (page 33), **Fried Chicken** (page 61), **Smoked Turkey Legs** (page 107), **Twice-Baked Sweet Potatoes** (page 109)

¼ cup salt
2 tablespoons ground smoked paprika
1 tablespoon ground coriander
1 tablespoon garlic powder
4 teaspoons ground cayenne pepper

1. Combine all the ingredients in an airtight container.

ORANGE AND LIME ROSEMARY SALT

Though the ingredients are simple, this salt combination brightens flavor and elevates any dish it's sprinkled on, making the food seem fancier than it actually is.

🛡 Difficulty: Easy

🕐 Prep time: 30 minutes

🔥 Cook time: 1 hour

⚠ Yield: ½ cup

🗻 Used in: Buttermilk Biscuits (page 57), Duck Poutine (page 97)

2 oranges, zested
4 limes, zested
1 tablespoon black peppercorns
3 sprigs fresh rosemary, stemmed
⅓ cup salt

1. Preheat oven to 170°F. Mix the orange zest, lime zest, peppercorns, and rosemary leaves together on a baking sheet. Place in the oven for 35 minutes, or until the citrus is dry but not burnt.

2. Remove from the oven and allow to cool. Transfer to a spice grinder (or a mortar and pestle), and blend 10 to 20 seconds, until the peppercorns are well ground. Place in a bowl, and combine with salt. Place in an airtight container, and store for up to 4 months.

VANILLA CINNAMON SALT

This mixture is just wonderful, especially for all the sweets I love to pass around during the Dawning. It reminds me a bit of snow, but it tastes far better.

🛡 Difficulty: Easy

🕐 Prep time: 15 minutes

⚠ Yield: ¼ cup

🗻 Used in: Chocolate Palmiers (page 167), Alkane Dragée Cookies (page 197)

1 vanilla bean
¼ cup salt
½ teaspoon ground cinnamon

1. Split the vanilla bean in half, and scrape the seeds out of the pod. Transfer the seeds into a bowl, and add the salt and ground cinnamon. Mix together until the vanilla seeds are evenly distributed. Place in an airtight container, and store for up to 4 months.

SHICHIMI TOGARASHI

⚔ **Difficulty: Easy**
🕐 **Prep time: 30 minutes**
🔥 **Cook time: 1 hour**
⚠ **Yield:** ½ cup
🍲 **Used in:** **Gyoza** (page 73), **Spicy Ramen** (page 75), **Bulgogi Burritos** (page 87)

In my review of reports about Mars, one description stuck with me as it described the planet in a way I never imagined: "So red as if it were ablaze, yet so cold. Eerie and chaotic, yet familiar and welcoming." Whenever I make a batch of shichimi togarashi, a spice popular in pre-Collapse Japanese cuisine, I can't help but think of that.

2 oranges, zested
1 teaspoon Sichuan peppercorns
1 teaspoon black peppercorns
⅓ cup red pepper flakes
2 teaspoons white sesame seeds
2 teaspoons black sesame seeds
1 sheet nori
2 teaspoons garlic powder

1. Preheat oven to 170°F. Mix the orange zest and both peppercorns together on a baking sheet. Place in the oven for 35 minutes, or until the orange is dry but not burnt.

2. Remove from the oven and allow to cool. Place the orange zest and both peppercorns along with the red pepper flakes, both types of sesame seeds, and nori in a spice grinder (or a mortar and pestle), and blend 10 to 20 seconds, until the peppercorns are well ground. Transfer to a bowl and mix together with the garlic powder. Place in an airtight container, and store for up to 4 months.

SHALLOT VINAIGRETTE

⚔ **Difficulty: Easy**

🕐 **Prep time: 45 minutes**

⚠ **Yield:** ½ cup

⬢ **Used in:** Salmon Quinoa Bowl (page 45)

Out of all the recipes in this book, this one may be the oldest. I happened upon it while reviewing some archives about the Clovis Bray Institute. Someone had scribbled a few notes about a salad they were served during a meeting to try later.

3 small shallots, minced
3 tablespoons lemon juice
1 tablespoon lemon zest
3 tablespoons rice vinegar
½ tablespoon sugar
⅔ cup olive oil
Salt and pepper

1. Combine the shallots, lemon juice, lemon zest, rice vinegar, and sugar in a medium-size mixing bowl. Let sit for 20 minutes to allow the flavors to mingle. Vigorously whisk the olive oil into the mixture, and season with salt and pepper to your liking. Use immediately, or store the dressing in an airtight container in the refrigerator for up to one week. The oil and acid will separate after sitting for a while, so make sure to shake vigorously before serving.

GOCHUJANG TOMATILLO SALSA

🏅 **Difficulty: Medium**
🕐 **Prep time: 45 minutes**
⚠ **Yield: 3 cups**
📦 **Used in: Bulgogi Burritos** (page 87)

*I had a meeting a while ago to discuss the public events taking place next year and decided to bring snacks for the group. But you can bet any dish I make won't be a simple plate of chips and dip. Tsk. As Tess would say: I'll bring salsa . . . with **style!***

7 tomatillos, halved and husks removed
5 cloves garlic, peeled
1 jalapeño, halved and seeds removed
½ yellow onion
¼ cup fresh cilantro
3 scallions, trimmed
2 to 3 tablespoons gochujang, per desired
   spice level
Juice of 2 limes
1 teaspoon salt
1 teaspoon pepper

1. Preheat oven broiler. Place the tomatillos, garlic, jalapeño, and onion on a baking sheet. Put the baking sheet under the broiler, and cook until the tomatillos have charred slightly. This should take about 10 minutes, but check occasionally to make sure the ingredients aren't completely burnt.

2. Remove from the oven, and allow to cool. Transfer to a food processor. Add the cilantro, scallions, gochujang, lime juice, salt, and pepper.

3. Pulse in the food processor until smooth. Season with additional salt and pepper if needed. This can be stored in an airtight container in the refrigerator for up to 1 week.

PICKLED VEGETABLES

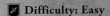
Difficulty: Easy

Prep time: 30 minutes

Yield: 1 cup

Used in:
Banh Mi Burgers
(page 83)

During the Golden Age, there was such an abundance of produce that they needed to find ways to preserve fresh vegetables. This quick recipe creates tangy vegetables that can be enjoyed as a snack or as condiments with other foods.

½ cup rice vinegar

2 cups warm water

¼ cup sugar

2 tablespoons salt

2 carrots, peeled and julienned

1 small daikon radish, julienned

1. Combine the rice vinegar, warm water, sugar, and salt in a large container with a lid, and stir or whisk to dissolve the sugar and salt. Add the carrots and daikon radish into the container. If the carrots and daikon are not fully submerged, add additional rice vinegar.

2. Seal the lid of the container and place in the refrigerator for at least 4 hours. The longer they are left to pickle, the more flavorful the carrots and daikon will become. This can be stored in the refrigerator for about 2 weeks.

TAKEN BUTTER

I came up with this recipe as a joke to lift the spirits of the Guardians when they returned from their travels. My timing was a little off, but the flavor of the butter was spot-on.

- Difficulty: Easy
- Prep time: 20 minutes
- Rest time: 2 hours
- Yield: 1 log
- Used in: Banh Mi Burgers (page 83)

1 cup unsalted butter, softened
1 teaspoon salt
2 teaspoons pepper
1 head black garlic, peeled
1 scallion, green portion only, finely chopped

1. Combine all the ingredients in a bowl. Mix until all ingredients just come together. Transfer the mixture onto a sheet of plastic wrap. Using plastic wrap, shape the butter into a log. Wrap completely in plastic wrap. Refrigerate for at least 2 hours before serving. The butter can be stored in the refrigerator for up to 2 weeks.

DASHI STOCK

This was one of the quintessential recipes of many Japanese restaurants back during the Golden Age. The ramen shop in the Tower goes through at least twenty-five batches a day.

- Difficulty: Medium
- Prep time: 4 hours
- Cook time: 15 minutes
- Yield: 3 cups
- Used in: Spicy Ramen (page 75), French Onion Soup (page 141)

One 4-by-4-inch piece kombu
3 cups water
1 cup dried bonito flakes

1. Place the kombu in a quart-size pot with the water. Allow it to rest for 4 hours.

2. After the kombu has soaked, place the pot over medium heat. Right before the water comes to a boil, remove the kombu. Add the bonito flakes, and simmer for 15 minutes. Remove the pot from the heat, and let it sit for 5 minutes. Strain through a mesh strainer. The stock can be stored in an airtight container in the refrigerator for up to 5 days.

CHICKEN BROTH

Difficulty: Medium

Prep time: 1 hour and 15 minutes

Cook time: 4 hours

Yield: 2 quarts

Used in: Avgolemono (page 41), **Tortilla Chicken Soup** (page 177)

If there's one thing I miss about the Farm, it's how accessible fresh poultry was. Nowadays, I make this dish less often. It's delicious, but I swear the Colonel gives me looks of disapproval any time I make this. Can't say I blame her, but you can't please everyone.

1 whole chicken

2 tablespoons Lemon Garlic Pepper Salt (page 18)

1 yellow onion, quartered

2 leeks, halved

4 celery ribs, cut into large chunks

2 carrots, cut into large chunks

2 dried bay leaves

2 sprigs fresh oregano

2½ quarts water

1. Preheat oven to 400°F. Rub the whole chicken inside and out with the Lemon Garlic Pepper Salt. Place the chicken, onion, leeks, celery, and carrots in a 7.25-quart oven-safe pot or Dutch oven, and roast, uncovered, for 1 hour and 15 minutes, or longer, until the chicken is cooked.

2. Remove the pot from the oven, and let cool until the chicken can be handled. Take the chicken out of the pot and remove the chicken breast—setting aside the skin—and shred. Place the meat in the refrigerator, covered, for use in other recipes.

3. Break down the rest of the chicken by removing the limbs and splitting the chest cavity with a chef's knife. Return the chicken parts, including the skin, to the pot with the roasted vegetables, then add the bay leaves, oregano, and water.

4. Bring the pot to a boil over medium-high heat, then reduce the heat to low. Keep at a slight simmer for 4 hours. Make sure to occasionally add water to keep the water level consistent. After the broth has simmered for 4 hours, carefully strain the pot into another container to separate the broth from all the ingredients. The stock can be stored in an airtight container in the refrigerator for up to 5 days.

MARSHMALLOWS

⚔ **Difficulty: Medium**

🕐 **Prep time: 30 minutes**

🔥 **Cook time: 30 minutes**

⚠ **Yield: One 9-by-13-inch sheet**

🗺 **Used in: S'mores Bark** (page 127)

Sometimes the Traveler reminds me of a big marshmallow, floating in the sky. I'm all too aware it wouldn't taste like one, but the thought can be comforting. I've heard, at least, that it smells faintly of vanilla on the inside.

2½ tablespoons unflavored gelatin
1 cup cold water, divided
2 cups sugar
½ cup light corn syrup
¼ teaspoon salt
1½ teaspoons vanilla extract
Confectioners' sugar, for topping

1. Combine the gelatin and ½ cup of the cold water in the bowl of a stand mixer fitted with a whisk attachment, and set aside.

2. In a medium-size pot over medium-high heat, combine the other ½ cup cold water, sugar, corn syrup, and salt. Stir together and use a candy thermometer to watch the temperature. Cook until the mixture reaches 240°F. Remove from heat, and turn the stand mixer to low.

3. Slowly pour the hot sugar mixture into the stand mixer while it's running. Turn the mixer to high, and mix for 10 to 15 minutes, or until it thickens—the mixture should become very fluffy and somewhat stiff. Near the end, add the vanilla extract.

4. Prepare a 9-by-13-inch pan by spraying with nonstick spray and sprinkling liberally with confectioners' sugar to make sure the marshmallows will release from the pan.

5. Transfer the sugar mixture into the pan, and spread evenly. Sprinkle the top with additional confectioners' sugar. Allow the marshmallows to rest, uncovered, overnight. Use an oiled knife to cut the marshmallows to your desired size; then use a sieve filled with additional confectioners' sugar to evenly dust each side again so the marshmallows don't stick to one another. The marshmallows can be stored in an airtight container at room temperature for up to 2 weeks.

THE TOWER: THE BAZAAR

There's something wonderful about standing among other vendors selling their goods, and I love seeing people go about their days in a place that has only recently returned to normalcy. It shows the strength of everyone here—Human, Exo, and Awoken; Guardian and non-Guardian alike—in remembering the past but moving toward a better future. And I just adore the view up here!

I'm not the only one who loves the view from the Tower. I often run into Ikora Rey, the Warlock Vanguard, who always has something on her mind. She likes to walk the Bazaar, greeting passersby as she goes, and she always offers a hand when I bring in new goods for the locals. But she is always glancing out among the scattered pieces of the Traveler, as if she's still looking for answers, knowing they have to be out there somewhere.

I'm but a simple woman, here to lift the spirits of those in the Tower. I don't have answers to every question. I'm not even sure if every question has an answer, but I know that every stomach has a craving, and shopping in the Bazaar can really amplify that craving. The ancient texts from the Golden Age refer to bazaars as wonderful places where shoppers roamed from stall to stall with food in hand, shopping, gossiping, and just enjoying life. The food served there was easy to eat on the go and referred to as "street food." Because I'd like to bring some of this back to the Tower, I have put together a nice list of recipes to enjoy. Make these with friends and sample everything, or keep it all to yourself!

KEFTA

- Difficulty: Easy
- Prep time: 1½ hours
- Cook time: 20 minutes
- Yield: 10 skewers
- Dietary notes: Dairy-Free

These delicious meat skewers are packed with protein and great for people on the go, as so many people in the Bazaar often are. They're easy to hold onto as you walk through the market, looking for that perfect acquisition.

10 bamboo skewers

2 shallots, peeled

4 cloves garlic, peeled

3 tablespoons fresh parsley leaves

3 tablespoons fresh cilantro leaves

10 fresh mint leaves

2½ pounds ground lamb

3 tablespoons Spicy Smoked Paprika Salt (page 18)

1 tablespoon ground fennel seed

Olive oil

1. Soak the bamboo skewers in water for at least 30 minutes

2. Place the shallots, garlic, parsley, cilantro, and mint leaves in a food processor. Process until the ingredients are finely chopped. Transfer to a large bowl. Add the ground lamb, Spicy Smoked Paprika Salt, and ground fennel seed. Combine until the ingredients just come together, but do not overwork the meat.

3. Divide the meat into 10 portions, forming each into a 4-inch-long log around a bamboo skewer. Repeat with the remaining skewers and portions. Place on a tray with parchment paper. Lightly brush each of the keftas with olive oil. Cover with plastic wrap, and refrigerate for at least 1 hour.

4. Grill the kefta over medium-high heat for about 5 to 10 minutes, flipping occasionally, until all sides are evenly browned.

GAMBAS AL AJILLO

Difficulty: Easy
Prep time: 1 hour
Cook time: 10 minutes
Yield: 4 servings
Dietary notes: Shellfish; Dairy-Free

Back during the Golden Age, the oceans of Earth teemed with fish and other marine creatures, and a recipe like this was easy to make. These days it takes a bit more effort to attain shrimp, but this recipe deserves to be preserved for future generations as the Guardians continue to fight for the future of our world.

1 baguette

1½ pounds shrimp, shelled, cleaned, and tails left on

2 tablespoons Spicy Smoked Paprika Salt (page 18)

½ cup plus 3 tablespoons olive oil, divided

10 cloves garlic, minced

Juice and zest of 1 lemon

¼ cup fresh parsley leaves, chopped

Salt and pepper

1. Preheat oven to 400°F. Slice the baguette, and set on a baking sheet.

2. Combine the shrimp and Spicy Smoked Paprika Salt in a bowl, and let rest for 10 minutes.

3. While the shrimp is resting, bake the baguettes on one side for 4 minutes. Flip and bake for another 4 minutes. Turn off the oven, but leave the baguettes in the oven to keep warm while you make the shrimp.

4. Add ½ cup of the olive oil to a large frying pan over low heat. Add the minced garlic, and cook until the garlic becomes fragrant and just begins to brown. Add the shrimp, and cook until they turn pink, about 2 to 3 minutes. Remove from heat, and add the lemon zest, lemon juice, and parsley. Season with salt and pepper to taste.

5. Remove from oven, and brush each side with the 3 tablespoons of olive oil, then serve alongside the shrimp.

LAMB TAGINE

- **Difficulty: Medium**
- **Prep time: 45 minutes**
- **Cook time: 90 minutes**
- **Yield: 6 servings**
- **Dietary notes: Dairy-Free**

When I'm spending my free time putting together a new outfit, I love slow-cooked recipes that gradually build up spice and flavor without needing too much attention. The lamb in this recipe can be hard to come by in the Tower, but it's worth the trouble to find.

1 tablespoon garam masala

1 tablespoon ground cumin

1 teaspoon ground turmeric

2 teaspoons ground coriander

2 teaspoons ground fennel seeds

1 teaspoon pepper

2 teaspoons salt

2 pounds boneless lamb shoulder, cut into 1-inch cubes

2 tablespoons canola oil, plus more if needed

½ red onion, sliced

5 cloves garlic, minced

Pinch of saffron (optional)

1 cinnamon stick

2 dried bay leaves

2 tablespoons tomato paste

1 sweet potato, peeled and cut into chunks

½ cup golden raisins

2 to 4 cups Chicken Broth (page 25)

1 bunch fresh cilantro, chopped

3 scallions, chopped

1. Combine the garam masala, cumin, turmeric, coriander, fennel seeds, pepper, and salt in a large bowl. Add the lamb cubes to the bowl and toss until the meat is completely coated in the spices.

2. Place a Dutch oven over medium heat, and add 1 tablespoon of the canola oil. Add a single layer of the lamb to cook in batches. Do not over-crowd the pan. Brown all sides of the meat. Remove and place on a plate. Add additional canola oil, if needed, and continue this process until all the lamb has been browned.

3. Add an additional tablespoon of canola oil to the Dutch oven. Add the red onion, and cook until softened. Add the garlic, saffron, cinnamon stick, bay leaves, tomato paste, sweet potato, golden raisins, and lamb. Stir everything to combine. Add enough broth to just barely cover every-thing, and stir together well. Bring to a boil, and then reduce the heat to low. Partly cover, and let simmer for 75 to 90 minutes, or until the lamb is tender. Serve with the Roasted Vegetable Couscous Salad (page 37).

ROASTED VEGETABLE COUSCOUS SALAD

- ⚔ **Difficulty:** Easy
- 🕐 **Prep time:** 1 hour
- 🔥 **Cook time:** 1 hour
- ⚠ **Yield:** 5 servings
- 🏕 **Dietary notes:** Vegan

This simple salad is light and filled with fresh vegetables. Though I can reliably find this dish in the Bazaar, its bright vegetables remind me of my time on the Farm, surrounded by greenery.

2 zucchini, cut into ½-inch slices

1 yellow squash, cut into ½-inch slices

1 red bell pepper, cut into ½-inch pieces

¼ red onion, thinly sliced

8 cloves garlic, sliced

¼ cup plus 2 tablespoons olive oil, divided

1 teaspoon salt

1 teaspoon pepper

2 cups vegetable broth

1½ cups pearl couscous

1 tablespoon dried oregano

2 teaspoons garlic powder

1 teaspoon dried thyme

One 15-ounce can artichoke hearts, drained and quartered

1. Preheat oven to 425°F. Combine the zucchini, yellow squash, red bell pepper, red onion, and garlic cloves in a medium bowl. Add 2 tablespoons of the olive oil, and toss together.

2. Prepare a baking sheet with aluminum foil and nonstick spray. Place the mixed vegetables on the baking sheet. Season with salt and pepper. Bake for 20 to 25 minutes, or until the vegetables have browned. Remove from the oven, and set aside to cool.

3. Place the vegetable broth in a saucepan over medium-high heat. Bring to a boil. Turn off the heat, add couscous, and cover. Allow to rest for 15 minutes. Uncover, and check to see if the couscous is cooked through and tender. Drain any remaining liquid in the pan. Transfer to a large bowl. Add the remaining ¼ cup of olive oil, oregano, garlic powder, thyme, and additional salt and pepper to taste, then toss together lightly. Add the roasted vegetables and artichoke hearts. Mix until just combined. Can be served warm or cold.

INVECTIVE

- Difficulty: Easy
- Prep time: 1 hour
- Yield: 1 pitcher
- Dietary notes: Vegan

This sangria recipe reminds me of Ikora in so many ways: powerful, elegant, and clad in a swirl of red and purple. I do absolutely love her robe; it has such beautiful fabric. After all, she got it from the best Outfitter in the Tower.

One 750-ml bottle red wine
½ cup maraschino liquour
½ cup triple sec liqueur
1 cup cherry juice
1 cup orange juice
1 orange, sliced
2 cups fresh cherries, pitted
    and halved
2 limes, sliced

1. Combine all the ingredients in a pitcher, and stir together. Refrigerator for at least 1 hour. Serve over ice with extra fruit if desired.

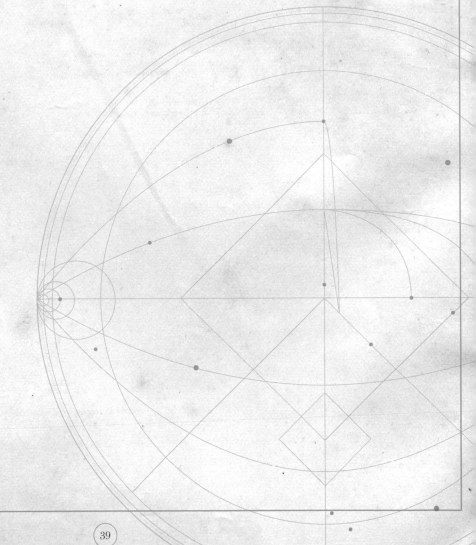

AVGOLEMONO

- Difficulty: Medium
- Prep time: 2 hours
- Cook time: 6 hours
- Yield: 6 bowls
- Dietary notes: Eggs; Dairy-Free

This soup is just like the brave people of the Tower. It may appear simple and straightforward, but the punch of flavor is anything but.

1 yellow onion, finely chopped

2 tablespoons olive oil

2 cloves garlic, minced

2 quarts Chicken Broth (page 25)

Salt and pepper

¾ cup arborio rice

2 whole eggs

1 egg yolk

1 cup lemon juice

2 tablespoons lemon zest

2 teaspoons Lemon Garlic Pepper Salt (page 18)

One medium chicken breast, cooked and shredded

Fresh parsley, chopped

1. In a large pot over medium-low heat, add the onion and olive oil. Cook until the onion has softened and turned a light golden brown, about 10 to 15 minutes. Add the garlic, and cook for 2 minutes. Increase the heat to medium-high, then pour in the chicken broth and bring to a slight boil. Season with salt and pepper to taste. Reduce the heat back to medium-low, and add the arborio rice. Cook until the rice is very tender, about 35 to 40 minutes.

2. In a bowl, whisk together the eggs, lemon juice, lemon zest, and Lemon Garlic Pepper Salt. Slowly introduce the hot broth into the lemon egg mixture. Make sure to do this slowly (about a half cup at a time), and continuously whisk to avoid cooking the eggs too quickly. Repeat this process 4 more times to heat up the egg mixture. Pour and whisk into the pot with the rest of the broth.

3. Reduce the heat to low, and whisk slightly until the soup has thickened. Taste and season with salt and pepper once again. Add the shredded chicken. Cook until the chicken has heated up, and serve garnished with parsley.

PITA BREAD

⬙ Difficulty: Medium

⏱ Prep time: 3 hours

🔥 Cook time: 5 minutes per disc

⚠ Yield: 10 pitas

▨ Dietary notes: Dairy-Free; Vegan

I've heard tales of the awful Hive and their pocket space magic or whatever the youths are calling it these days. I don't know what to make of it, but the only pocket I need when I'm visiting the Bazaar is this pita recipe.

1 cup warm water

2 tablespoons olive oil, plus more for oiling the bowl

1 teaspoon salt

1 tablespoon sugar

2¼ teaspoons active dry yeast

2 cups all-purpose flour

¾ cup whole wheat flour

2 teaspoons garlic powder

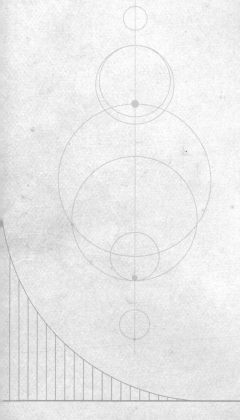

1. Combine the water, olive oil, salt, sugar, and yeast in the bowl of a stand mixer. Mix well, and set aside for 10 minutes to allow the yeast to get frothy. Combine the all-purpose flour, wheat flour, and garlic powder in a bowl.

2. Add ⅓ of the flour mixture to the yeast bowl, and mix with the dough attachment. Mix at low speed until the dough just starts to come together. Add another third of the flour mixture, and keep mixing. Repeat with the last third, and mix until the dough is smooth and tacky. If the dough is too sticky, add 1 tablespoon of all-purpose flour until it becomes tacky. Knead the dough for 5 minutes.

3. Transfer the dough ball into a bowl that has been coated with about a tablespoon of olive oil, and turn the dough over until all sides are coated in oil. Cover the bowl with plastic wrap, and let the dough rest at room temperature until it has doubled in size, about 2 hours.

4. Lightly flour a clean counter or work surface, and place the dough on the counter. Lightly pat down the dough to deflate it, then divide it into 10 equal pieces. Gently form each of the pieces into a round ball. Cover the pieces of dough with a towel, and let rest for 30 minutes.

5. Working on a lightly floured countertop, take a ball and pat it down with your hands. With a rolling pin, roll out into a 6-inch disc. Prepare a plate with a large kitchen towel on top.

6. Place a skillet over medium-high heat. Make sure the skillet is hot. Take a rolled-out piece of dough, and flip it onto the skillet. Cook until the disc begins to puff up or the bottom turns golden brown, about 2 to 3 minutes. Flip and repeat on the other side, about 2 minutes. Place the cooked pita on the kitchen towel and wrap. Repeat with the remaining discs.

7. To store, remove the pitas from the towel after they have cooled and place them into a ziplock bag. They will remain fresh for up to 4 days.

Difficulty: Medium
Prep time: 4 hours
Cook time: 45 minutes
Yield: 4 servings
Dietary notes: Dairy-Free

SALMON QUINOA BOWL

Reading about the last days on Kraken Mare on Titan, I was struck by how farmed salmon was available there, even on those far-off platforms over the roiling methane sea. The Golden Age was truly a marvel. This delightful recipe makes use of the salmon we still have here on Earth—for which I'm quite thankful.

Salmon:

¼ cup honey
⅓ cup olive oil
1 teaspoon dried oregano
1 teaspoon dried thyme
2 teaspoons salt
1 teaspoon black pepper
Zest and juice of 2 lemons
4 cloves garlic, minced
1 pound salmon, split into 4 equal pieces

Quinoa:

1½ cups quinoa
3 cups vegetable broth
1 cinnamon stick
1 teaspoon salt
3 teaspoons chia seeds
2 scallions, chopped
1 teaspoon fresh dill, chopped
2 teaspoons fresh mint, chopped
2 teaspoons fresh cilantro, chopped
2 tablespoons olive oil

Toppings:

2 small cucumbers, sliced
1 avocado, sliced
10 grape tomatoes, sliced
¼ cup feta cheese (optional)
15 kalamata olives, quartered
7 radishes, sliced
Shallot Vinaigrette (page 21)

For the salmon:

1. Combine the honey, olive oil, oregano, thyme, salt, pepper, lemon zest, lemon juice, and garlic in an airtight container. Add the salmon, and marinate for at least 1 hour but no more than 3 hours.

2. Preheat oven to 400°F. Prepare a baking sheet with aluminum foil and nonstick spray. Place the marinated salmon on the baking sheet, and bake for 15 to 18 minutes, until the salmon reaches an internal temperature of 140°F.

For the quinoa:

3. Combine the quinoa, vegetable broth, cinnamon stick, and salt in a pot over medium-high heat. Bring to a boil, then reduce the heat to low-medium. Cover and simmer for about 15 minutes, or until the liquid has evaporated. Keep covered, and let it rest for 5 minutes.

4. Transfer the quinoa to a bowl, and combine with the chia seeds, scallions, dill, mint, cilantro, and olive oil.

For the toppings:

5. Split the quinoa into 4 serving bowls. Top each bowl with a salmon fillet and a portion of the toppings. Top with a splash of the Shallot Vinaigrette.

WAVESPLITTER

Difficulty: Medium

Prep time: 30 minutes

Cook time: 15 minutes

Inactive time: 3 hours

Yield: 1 pitcher of lemonade, 5 mixed drinks

Dietary notes: Vegan

I've never been to Titan, but I've admired videos of the rolling blue-green oceans that cover the moon. I'd love to visit it someday, but until then I'll have to settle for this pleasant drink inspired by the color of those seas.

½ cup sugar
2½ cups water, divided
20 fresh mint leaves
½ cup fresh lemon juice
   (about 3 to 5 lemons)
2 tablespoons curaçao
1 tablespoon melon liqueur
Ice cubes
Mint sprigs

1. Combine sugar and ½ cup of the water in a saucepan, and place over medium-high heat. Whisk until the sugar has dissolved, and bring to a boil. Reduce the heat, and let simmer for 5 minutes. Remove the syrup from the heat, and allow to cool to room temperature.

2. Muddle the mint leaves in a pitcher. Add the syrup, lemon juice, and 2 cups water. Mix together. Store in the refrigerator for at least 3 hours before serving. Can be stored in the refrigerator for up to 7 days.

3. When ready to serve, combine the lemonade, curacao, and melon liqueur in a cocktail shaker with ice. Cover and shake vigorously for 10 seconds. Strain and pour into a glass. Serve with a mint sprig.

IKORA REY AND OSIRIS

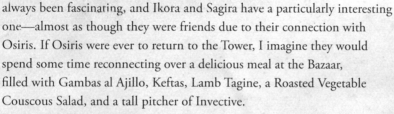

Some newer arrivals to the Last City may see Ikora as a champion of study, of measured response, and of strong, stoic leadership, but I've seen the records. She used to spend her days roughing up other Guardians in the Crucible, and as Shaxx puts it, she was *quite* good at it, too. Beyond her physical prowess, she's known for her thirst for knowledge, which she developed while working with her former mentor, Osiris.

Ikora mentioned recently that she had heard from Osiris. She has described him as someone who can't seem to sit in one place, or time, for very long. I can't help but think some Kefta skewers would be perfect for a restless person like that. Whenever Ikora speaks of her old mentor, she always mentions her interactions with Sagira. The relationship between Guardians and Ghosts has always been fascinating, and Ikora and Sagira have a particularly interesting one—almost as though they were friends due to their connection with Osiris. If Osiris were ever to return to the Tower, I imagine they would spend some time reconnecting over a delicious meal at the Bazaar, filled with Gambas al Ajillo, Keftas, Lamb Tagine, a Roasted Vegetable Couscous Salad, and a tall pitcher of Invective.

THE TOWER: THE HANGAR

The Hangar is one of my favorite locations in the Tower. I love walking across the catwalks and watching all the workers go about their day "sewing" metal to machines and creating technological marvels. Sometimes I'll catch an engineer on break and ask them about the work they've been doing. They often go on and on about all sorts of technical details that I can't even begin to understand, but I love listening to people talk about their passion for their craft. It motivates me to keep pushing forward with my own work.

Of all the workers in the Hangar, no one is as motivated as Amanda Holliday. She arrived at the Last City all by herself at a very young age. Zavala fortunately recognized her talents and interest in machinery and gave her the resources and tools necessary to become one of the best shipwrights in the Tower—and one of the best pilots, too. Despite her talent for flying, she's very down-to-earth and always makes time to show me around when I stop by as she is driven to help everyone around her.

I was shocked when Amanda showed me something she found while sorting through her possessions. Among the heirlooms from her time on the road with her parents—beside a beautifully crafted shotgun—was a series of recipes, passed down from ages ago. I had no idea this sort of cooking existed before! These comfort meals, meant to fill the stomach and the soul after a hard day of work, were a perfect addition to my collection of recipes. I immediately ran back home to put them to the test. They were so delicious that I ended up eating far more than intended and could barely muster the energy to call Amanda and give her the good news. Be careful not to overdo it with these delicious meals unless you don't have anything else on your schedule.

HUSH PUPPIES

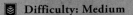

- **Difficulty: Medium**
- **Prep time: 30 minutes**
- **Cook time: 5 minutes per batch**
- **Yield: 24 to 28 hush puppies**
- **Dietary notes: Dairy**

One old story says the comfort food hush puppies got their name because of their ability to quickly quiet a hungry, growling stomach. I think that's just what these tireless comrades in the Hangar need—if only they would stop working long enough to take a bite.

1¼ cups cornmeal

¾ cup all-purpose flour

2 tablespoons sugar

1 tablespoon Lemon Garlic Pepper Salt (page 18)

½ teaspoon cayenne pepper

2 teaspoons baking powder

2 small jalapeños, seeds removed and finely chopped

4 scallions, white and light green parts only, finely chopped

1 cup shredded cheddar cheese

1 egg

1 cup buttermilk

2 tablespoons unsalted butter, melted and cooled

Peanut oil, for frying

Ranch dressing, for dipping

1. Combine the cornmeal, flour, sugar, Lemon Garlic Pepper Salt, cayenne pepper, baking powder, jalapeños, scallions, and cheddar cheese in a large bowl. In a separate small bowl, thoroughly combine the egg, buttermilk, and melted butter. Pour the liquid ingredients into the dry ingredients, and whisk until just combined. Set aside.

2. Fill a large and deep heavy pot with 2 inches of peanut oil, and bring to 360°F over medium-high heat. Use a 1-tablespoon scoop or spoon to create balls of batter. Carefully place balls in the hot oil, about 8 to 12 at a time; but do not overcrowd the pot—the balls should not touch. Fry until golden brown, turning constantly, about 4 to 5 minutes. Transfer to a plate covered with a paper towel to drain. Repeat with the rest of the batter. Serve with ranch dressing.

WHITE SAUSAGE GRAVY

◻ Difficulty: Easy
◷ Prep time: 10 minutes
◉ Cook time: 15 minutes
△ Yield: 3½ cups
◻ Dietary notes: Dairy

Amanda Holliday is one of the most gifted mechanics in the Tower. Her ability to fix and maintain any technology—whether it be some ancient Golden Age schematic pulled from an engram or a new ship engine design—is one of the main reasons the Tower is still a safe haven for all humanity. As Amanda has spent most of her time in the Hangar, her culinary skills are not quite up to par with her shipbuilding skills, so I provided her with this simple, hearty recipe.

2 cups whole milk

1 cup buttermilk

1 pound bulk country
   breakfast sausage

3 tablespoons unsalted butter

⅓ cup all-purpose flour

1 teaspoon garlic powder

1 to 2 tablespoons pepper

Salt

1. Combine the whole milk and buttermilk in a bowl, and set aside. Place a large fry pan over medium-high heat. Add nonstick spray or olive oil to the pan, then add the sausage. Break the sausage into chunks, and cook until brown, about 10 to 12 minutes. Remove the sausage meat to a plate or bowl, but leave the grease in the pan. Add the butter, and let melt. Whisk in the flour, and stir continuously for about 1 minute.

2. Reduce the heat to medium-low. Add the milk combination slowly while whisking constantly until the gravy has thickened, about 5 minutes. Return the sausage meat to the pan, and mix together. Add the garlic powder. Simmer for 5 minutes. If the gravy becomes too thick, add a splash of milk to reach your desired consistency. Season with pepper, and add salt to taste.

BUTTERMILK BISCUITS

- **Difficulty: Medium**
- **Prep time: 1½ hours**
- **Cook time: 13 to 16 minutes**
- **Yield: 12 biscuits**
- **Dietary notes: Dairy; Vegetarian**

Sometimes, on busy days, Amanda will request that I bring a few batches of biscuits to the Hangar to keep the workers' spirits up. This biscuit recipe is a simple and delicious one that will warm the soul, especially when paired with White Sausage Gravy!

3 cups all-purpose flour

1½ tablespoons sugar

2 teaspoons Orange and Lime Rosemary Salt (page 19)

1 tablespoon baking powder

¼ teaspoon baking soda

1 cup unsalted butter, cubed and chilled in the freezer for at least 20 minutes

1¼ cups buttermilk, chilled

2 tablespoons unsalted butter, melted

1. Combine flour, sugar, Orange and Lime Rosemary Salt, baking powder, and baking soda in a medium bowl. Add the cubed butter, and combine with your hands until it resembles coarse cornmeal. Place in the refrigerator, and let rest for 15 minutes.

2. Remove from the refrigerator, add the buttermilk, and stir until dough is slightly shaggy, about 3 minutes. Transfer to a floured countertop, and knead about 10 to 15 times, until the dough has come together and can be shaped into a rectangle.

3. Roll out the dough into a rectangle about 1 inch tall. Fold the dough into thirds, like you would fold a letter, by folding the top third of the dough toward you, then fold the bottom third over the first fold. Reroll the dough again, and fold the dough into thirds again. Reroll the dough once more, then cut into 12 equal pieces.

4. Preheat oven to 425°F. Place the pieces on a baking sheet lined with parchment paper. Place in the freezer for 20 minutes. Remove and brush each of the biscuits with melted butter. Bake for 15 to 20 minutes, or until golden brown. Transfer to a wire rack, and allow to cool.

CHICKEN-FRIED STEAK

🎖 Difficulty: Medium

🕐 Prep time: 45 minutes

🔥 Cook time: 4 to 6 minutes per piece

⚠ Yield: 4 servings

🔥 Dietary notes: Dairy; Eggs

If there's one thing the shipwrights in the Hanger love, it's a hearty meal. This delightful dish provides the team with a huge amount of energy after a long shift working on everything from jumpships to Wayfarer-class Sparrows.

4 cuts boneless beef top round steak (about ½ pound)

Salt and pepper

⅓ cup cornstarch

2 eggs

1 cup buttermilk

2½ cups all-purpose flour

1 tablespoon paprika

1 teaspoon garlic powder

1 teaspoon cayenne pepper

1. Prepare the beef by flattening each steak with a meat tenderizer to ¼-inch thick, and generously season both sides with salt and pepper to taste.

2. Set up three stations to bread the beef: On one plate, place the cornstarch. In a bowl, whisk the eggs with buttermilk. On a second plate, combine the flour, paprika, garlic powder, and cayenne pepper.

3. Coat one slice of beef with cornstarch. Dip the meat in the eggs, covering it completely, then let the excess drip off. Finally, coat with the flour mixture. Shake off any excess flour, and place on a wire rack. Repeat with the remaining portions. Let the steaks rest for 10 minutes.

4. Place a ½ inch of peanut oil in a deep pan. Heat the oil to about 325°F. Carefully fry the steaks for 2 to 3 minutes on each side, or until golden brown. Transfer to a plate with paper towels to drain. Serve with White Sausage Gravy (page 55) on top.

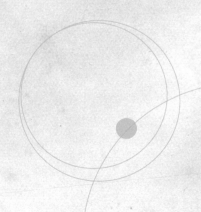

FRIED CHICKEN

- ⬡ **Difficulty: Hard**
- 🕐 **Prep time: 30 to 45 hours**
- 🔥 **Cook time: 10 to 18 minutes per batch**
- ⚠ **Yield: 8 servings**
- ⬚ **Dietary notes: Dairy**

Any time I'm dredging chicken to make my favorite guilty treat, I can't help but think of the tales of Dredgen Yor I've heard whispered among the Hangar's mechanics. I almost asked a friendly Exo if they thought the name was intentionally related to the action of coating food but thought better of it.

4 pounds bone-in chicken drumsticks, thighs, and wings

One 32-ounce jar of pickles, juice only

3 dried bay leaves

5 cloves garlic, smashed

2 tablespoons black peppercorns

1 quart buttermilk

Peanut oil, for frying

3 cups all-purpose flour

¼ cup Spicy Smoked Paprika Salt (page 18)

2 tablespoons salt

1 tablespoon pepper

2 tablespoons ground fennel seed

1. Combine the chicken pieces, pickle juice, bay leaves, garlic, and peppercorns in a large bowl. If the chicken is not completely covered by the brining liquid, add water until submerged. Cover and refrigerate for at least 24 hours, but no more than 48 hours.

2. Remove the chicken from the brine and pat dry. Transfer to another bowl with buttermilk. Cover and refrigerate for at least 3 hours.

3. Fill a large, deep heavy pot with 2 inches of peanut oil, and heat to 350°F over medium-high. Combine the flour, Spicy Smoked Paprika Salt, salt, pepper, and ground fennel in a medium bowl. When the oil has reached the target temperature, take a piece of chicken from the buttermilk and let any excess liquid drip off. Dredge in the spiced flour mixture until fully covered. Carefully place in the heated oil. Repeat with two to three more pieces of chicken, but do not overcrowd the pan or the oil temperature will drop too low.

4. Cook until the chicken reaches an internal temperature of 165°F:

Chicken drumsticks: 10 to 15 minutes

Chicken wings: 8 to 12 minutes

Chicken thighs: 12 to 18 minutes

5. Transfer to a plate covered with paper towels to rest and drain. Make sure to allow the oil to return to 350°F between each batch, then repeat with the remaining chicken.

COLESLAW

🗡 **Difficulty: Easy**

🕐 **Prep time: 10 hours**

⚠ **Yield: 8 servings**

▦ **Dietary notes:**
Eggs; Vegetarian

The first time I saw Xûr, I had spotted a suspicious figure huddled in the corner of the Hangar and was curious why they kept returning to the same spot. For a while, I was too unnerved to approach and introduce myself though I occasionally saw Guardians exchanging words and goods with him. Once, when he turned, I thought I saw a mask—or was it a beard, or maybe tentacles? As silly as this sounds, it reminded me of an old coleslaw recipe I like to bring to meetings at the Hangar. Eventually, Tess explained to me that he was Xûr and a Jovian and nothing to be afraid of. It took a while, but I became used to his presence—maybe next time I see him, I'll have built up the courage to offer him a helping of this coleslaw!

¾ cup mayonnaise

2 tablespoons Dijon mustard

1 tablespoon lemon juice

2 tablespoons apple cider vinegar

1 teaspoon celery salt

2 tablespoons sugar

2 cups green cabbage, core
removed and thinly sliced

2 cups red cabbage, core
removed and thinly sliced

¾ cup carrots, peeled and julienned

½ red onion, finely chopped

Salt and pepper

1. Whisk together the mayonnaise, Dijon mustard, lemon juice, apple cider vinegar, celery salt, and sugar in a small bowl. Combine the cabbages, carrot, and red onion in a large bowl. Toss in the dressing, and fully coat the vegetables. Cover and place in the refrigerator overnight. Add salt and pepper to taste.

TINCTURE OF QUEENSFOIL

- **Difficulty:** Easy
- **Prep time:** 12 hours
- **Cook time:** 45 minutes
- **Rest time:** At least 8 hours
- **Yield:** 8 servings
- **Dietary notes:** Vegan

I bumped into Guardians on their return from the Dreaming City and asked about a peculiar bottle in their possession. They called it a Tincture of Queensfoil. Its effects don't seem like something I need to experience, but the Guardians did mention that it tastes a bit like the blackberry tea that the Queen of the Reef loves so much, so I made myself a pitcher of this to hold me over.

9 cups water, divided
1½ cups sugar
8 ounces blackberries
3 Earl Grey tea bags
2 white tea bags
Additional blackberries, for garnish

1. Combine 1 cup of the water with the sugar and blackberries in a 2-quart saucepan, and place over medium-high heat. Stir until the sugar has dissolved, and then bring to a boil. Reduce the heat, and simmer for 15 minutes. Remove from the heat, and pour through a fine-mesh strainer into a pitcher.

2. Boil the remaining water in a large pot over medium-high. Add the Earl Grey and white tea bags, and turn off the heat. Let steep for 6 to 8 minutes. Remove the tea bags, transfer tea to the pitcher, and stir together. If you would like your tea to be slightly less sweet, add additional hot water.

3. Allow to cool completely, and then refrigerate overnight before serving. Serve in a glass with ice and fresh blackberries.

SUNSHOT

⚔ **Difficulty:** Easy

🕐 **Prep time:** 15 hours

🕐 **Rest time:** At least 8 hours

⚠ **Yield:** 2 servings

⬡ **Dietary notes:** Dairy

This pistol of a drink is just like the Exotic hand cannon it was named for. The bourbon, cinnamon, and nutmeg combine for a flavorful punch—just like Liu Feng's legendary Sunbreaker power.

½ cup bourbon

1 cinnamon stick

¼ teaspoon grated nutmeg

2 tablespoons honey

1 teaspoon vanilla extract

2 cups milk

1. Combine the bourbon, cinnamon stick, and grated nutmeg in a sealable bowl. Cover and let rest overnight. To make the punch, mix the spiced bourbon, honey, and vanilla extract in a cocktail shaker. Add ice and the milk. Cover and shake vigorously for 10 seconds. Strain and pour into a glass.

AMANDA HOLLIDAY
AND ZAVALA

If the Tower is the Human body, the Hangar is its heart. The workers there pour everything they have into keeping the fleets and Sparrows in top condition, doing their part to help the Guardians protect us. Even during the Dawning, the shifts remain long and the labor hard. But their leader, Amanda Holliday, ever driven to doggedly pursue what is right, tells me cheerfully, "There are always fifty things to do!" and returns to her work. Her crew follows her example, knowing their work is equally as important as the Guardians'.

Ever since she arrived at the Last City as an orphan, Amanda has been a hard worker. Zavala has taken it upon himself to keep her safe and supported, helping her become the leader she is today. But growth goes both ways: Amanda's kindness and empathy have rubbed off on Zavala as well. Though they are both busy and work long hours—one keeps an eye over the entire City, and the other builds ships and tinkers with any modification a Guardian may request (including adding stealth tech to Eris Morn's ship for a simple "test flight")—they always make a point to stop and share a hearty meal together. They often eat Amanda's favorite foods, such as warm Hush Puppies, Fried Chicken served with a Buttermilk Biscuit, a side of Coleslaw, and a Sunshot drink to round it all out.

CITY LIFE

The Last City isn't just the final point of defense for the Guardians defending humanity—it's also the only urban area left. Even with dangers afoot, the people living here need a place to walk around in the evening and relax. Scattered about are small shops and restaurants still in operation, but none are as iconic as the famous ramen shop. When the Cabal attacked, so much was lost that I was worried the City would never recover. Imagine my surprise when I returned to see a new ramen shop open for business. The owner was one of the many refugees we had snuck out of the occupied City, and they opened a new shop to celebrate getting back to life at the Tower. It was at this new location that I reunited with Cayde-6.

I'll never forget how kind Cayde was. I was absolutely devastated when I heard what happened at the Reef. I'm not sure how Cayde would have wanted to be commemorated, but I trust the Guardians to figure it out.

I've also made a tribute of my own: Because Cayde loved spending an evening out in the Tower—especially in the North Food District—I gathered some recipes inspired by life in the City in his honor. Despite not having the variety that cities during the Golden Age enjoyed, I took some of the most popular dishes here and mixed in a few ideas of my own to come up with a cosmopolitan set of recipes. I wanted to combine everything we have here so that anyone hosting friends and family can re-create a true City dining experience.

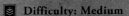

GYOZA

- **Difficulty: Medium**
- **Prep time: 3 hours**
- **Cook time: 10 to 15 minutes per batch**
- **Yield: 40 to 60 dumplings**
- **Dietary notes: Dairy-Free**

Everyone knows about the Tower ramen shop's signature Spicy Ramen, but you aren't getting the full experience unless you complement it with a beautiful plate of Gyoza. Fresh pork is imported from outside the city limits every day to make these delicious dumplings.

Dumplings:

½ head (about 400 grams) napa cabbage, thinly sliced

3 teaspoons salt, divided

1 pound ground pork

5 cloves garlic, minced

¼ cup water chestnuts, minced

1 tablespoon ginger, minced

3 scallions, diced

5 shiitake mushrooms, minced

2 teaspoons sesame oil

2 teaspoons soy sauce

1 teaspoon sake

½ tablespoon gochujang

2 teaspoons Shichimi Togarashi (page 20)

1 teaspoon sugar

1 package round gyoza wrappers

Water

Sauce:

¼ cup rice vinegar

3 tablespoons soy sauce

½ tablespoon sambal oelek (optional)

For the dumplings:

1. Place the sliced cabbage and 2 teaspoons of the salt in a strainer over a bowl, and allow to sit for at least 15 minutes, to remove excess water. Take the drained cabbage, and squeeze it to further remove excess water.

2. Combine the ground pork, drained cabbage, garlic, water chestnuts, ginger, scallions, and shiitake mushrooms in a medium bowl. Add the sesame oil, soy sauce, sake, gochujang, remaining salt, Shichimi Togarashi, and sugar. Thoroughly mix everything together.

3. Place a small bowl of water next to the area where you will be making the dumplings. Take a gyoza wrapper, and place 1 to 2 teaspoons of the filling in the center. Wet your index finger, then use it to wet the edges of the wrapper.

4. Fold the wrapper in half, and pinch the center together. Begin pleating one side of the wrapper, pressing firmly to seal it closed. Pleat the other side of the wrapper until the dumpling is completely sealed. Repeat with the remaining wrappers.

5. If you don't intend to eat all of the dumplings immediately, you can freeze and store them. Place on a baking sheet lined with parchment paper, and cover with plastic wrap. Place in the freezer for at least 30 minutes, then place all the gyoza in a sealable bag. The gyoza can be stored in the freezer for up to 2 months. When cooking the frozen dumplings, do not thaw them.

6. To cook the fresh dumplings, heat a large frying pan over medium-high heat with canola oil. Add a single layer of dumplings and cook until the bottoms brown slightly, about 1 to 2 minutes.

7. Add ½ cup of water and cover with a lid. Let the dumplings steam until they have cooked through and the water has completely evaporated. Remove the lid to let the bottoms crisp up slightly, another 1 to 2 minutes. Serve immediately.

For the sauce:

8. Combine soy sauce, rice vinegar, and sambal oelek. Add additional sambal oelek to make spicier.

SPICY RAMEN

- Difficulty: Medium
- Prep time: 1½ hours
- Cook time: 1 hour
- Yield: 4 servings
- Dietary notes: Dairy-Free

Spicy Ramen has been a staple here in the Tower for as long as I can remember. Highlighting an incredible combination of flavors and spices, this is one of the best recipes the Golden Age has to offer. Not even the Red Legion could bring down these golden noodles swimming in rich, flavorful broth.

Spiced Chicken.

3 tablespoons Shichimi Togarashi (page 20)
1 teaspoon salt
6 boneless, skin-on chicken thighs
2 teaspoons canola oil

Broth:

2 quarts Dashi Stock (page 24)
3 dried shiitake mushrooms, plus 10 fresh shiitake mushrooms, stems removed and sliced
3 teaspoons canola oil, divided
1 leek, white and light green parts only, diced
5 cloves garlic, minced
1½ cups kimchi, cut into bite-size pieces
2 tablespoons kimchi juice
1 tablespoon gochujang
3 tablespoons red miso
3 tablespoons soy sauce
Salt and pepper

Accompaniments:

4 pieces nori (optional)
4 servings ramen noodles, cooked
6 slices bacon, cooked and chopped
4 Ajitsuke Tamago (page 79), cut in half
3 scallions, sliced
Bean sprouts (optional)
Hot sauce (optional)

For the spiced chicken:

1. Combine Shichimi Togarashi and salt in a small bowl, and rub onto the chicken thighs.

2. Heat a pan with 2 teaspoons of canola oil over medium-high heat. Place the chicken thighs, skin-side down, and cook until it turns golden brown, about 5 to 8 minutes.

3. Flip and cook until the chicken is cooked all the way through, about 5 minutes. Transfer to a cutting board and allow to rest for 5 minutes. Cut into strips.

For the broth:

4. Place Dashi Stock with dried shiitake mushrooms in a 3-quart saucepan over medium-high heat. Bring to a simmer for 10 minutes. Remove the mushrooms. Set the broth aside.

5. Place a large pot with 2 teaspoons of the canola oil over medium-high heat. Add the fresh shiitake mushrooms, and cook until the edges are crispy, about 8 minutes. Transfer the mushrooms to a plate.

6. In the same pot, add another teaspoon of canola oil. Add the leeks and garlic, and cook until softened, about 3 minutes.

7. Add the kimchi, kimchi juice, gochujang, red miso, and soy sauce, and cook for about 4 minutes. Add the dashi broth and the crisped mushrooms. Bring to a simmer for 10 minutes. Season with salt and pepper if needed.

8. To serve, place a piece of nori on the side of a bowl and a serving of ramen noodles. Top with a portion of chicken thighs. Add a fourth of the cooked bacon in the center.

9. Add a fourth of the broth with vegetables. Top with 2 Ajitsuke Tamago halves, scallions, and bean sprouts. Top with additional hot sauce of your choice.

GYUDON

⚔ **Difficulty: Easy**

🕐 **Prep time: 45 minutes**

🔥 **Cook time: 30 minutes**

⚠ **Yield: 6 servings**

🖼 **Dietary notes:**
Dairy-Free

Believe it or not, the ramen shop actually used to sell a second entree: a simi-larly comforting dish that paired fluffy rice with beef that was simultaneously sweet and savory. Sadly, the shop doesn't sell this anymore because the fighting with the Fallen has created an ingredient shortage. So I've put together my own, just as delicious Gyudon recipe to share with everyone.

½ cup Dashi Stock (page 24)

3 tablespoons soy sauce

2 tablespoons sake

3 tablespoons mirin

3 tablespoons sugar

4 cloves garlic, minced

1½-inch piece fresh ginger, peeled
   and minced

1 yellow onion, thinly sliced

3 rib-eye steaks, very thinly sliced

3 cups rice, cooked

2 scallions, chopped

Pickled ginger

Sesame seeds

1. Combine the Dashi Stock, soy sauce, sake, mirin, sugar, garlic, and ginger in a medium pot over medium heat, and bring to a boil. Reduce the heat to low, and allow the sauce to simmer lightly for 10 minutes.

2. Return the heat to medium and add the onions. Cook the onions for about 10 to 15 minutes, or until they are soft and translucent.

3. Add the rib eye. Simmer for 5 to 8 minutes, or until the meat is just cooked.

4. To serve, place ½ cup of the cooked rice in a bowl, and top with the simmered beef and onions. Pour a small amount of the sauce over the beef. Top with scallions. Serve with pickled ginger and a sprinkle of sesame seeds.

AJITSUKE TAMAGO

- Difficulty: Easy
- Prep time: 20 minutes
- Cook time: 10 minutes
- Rest time: 24 hours
- Yield: 4 soft-boiled eggs
- Dietary notes: Eggs; Dairy-Free; Vegetarian

I've gotten a little spoiled when it comes to fresh ingredients, thanks to the time I spent recovering at the Farm. I love the Ajitsuke Tamago they serve at the ramen shop, but I know it would be even better if they had fresh eggs. I've politely asked the Colonel for some help, but she tilted her head at me and then walked away. I'll have to try again later.

4 eggs
½ cup soy sauce
¼ cup sugar
¼ cup mirin
¼ cup sake

1. Bring a pot of water to a boil. Gently place the eggs in the pot, cover, and cook for 6½ minutes. Once cooked, immediately take the pot off the stove and place under cold running water. Move the contents to a bowl with ice cubes and water. Carefully remove the shells from the eggs.

2. Mix the soy sauce, sugar, mirin, and sake in a sealable bag. Add the eggs. Seal and make sure the eggs are fully covered. Place in the refrigerator, and marinate for at least 24 hours. This dish can be stored in the refrigerator for up to three days.

ACE OF SPADES

⚔ Difficulty: Easy
🕐 Prep time: 10 minutes
⚠ Yield: 1 drink
▦ Dietary notes: Vegan

This recipe is reminiscent of the bright green nonalcoholic libation I often caught Cayde-6 drinking at a nearby bar. This drink is a little something I concocted to honor our lost friend, though I've added a little extra punch to this version. And what could be a better name than his trusty sidearm?

3 ounces melon liqueur
1 ounce white rum
1 ounce orange liqueur
2 ounces pineapple juice
½ ounce lime juice
½ ounce lemon juice

1. Fill a cocktail shaker with ice, and add all the ingredients. Shake thoroughly. Fill a highball glass with ice and pour the drink.

BANH MI BURGERS

⚔ **Difficulty:** Easy
🕐 **Prep time:** 45 minutes
🔥 **Cook time:** 30 minutes
⚠ **Yield:** 4 servings
▨ **Dietary notes:** None

I got this intriguing recipe from the Drifter, who created it back when he used to run a bar. With a particular combination of spice and savory flavors, these burgers kept his patrons guessing.

Pork Burgers:

2 tablespoons canola oil
1 shallot, minced
2 scallions, white and light green parts
   only, minced
1 pound ground pork
2 teaspoons ginger, grated
Zest of 1 lime
1 tablespoon fish sauce
1 teaspoon soy sauce
½ teaspoon sesame oil

For the Burgers:

4 buns
3 tablespoons Taken Butter (page 24)
Garlic powder
Mayonnaise
Pâté
1 cucumber, sliced
2 jalapeños, sliced
Cilantro
Pickled Vegetables (page 23)

For the pork burgers:

1. Place a pan over medium-high heat. Add 2 teaspoons canola oil, and cook the shallots and scallions until softened, about 5 minutes. Remove from the heat, and allow to cool completely.

2. Combine the cooled shallots and scallions, ground pork, ginger, lime zest, fish sauce, soy sauce, and sesame oil in a bowl until just combined. Shape into 4 equal patties.

3. Place a grill pan over medium-high heat. Cover the pan with nonstick spray, and place the patties on the pan. Cook for 4 minutes, flip, and cook for another 5 minutes, or until the patties reach an internal temperature of 160°F. Transfer to a plate, and let rest.

For serving:

4. Preheat oven broiler. Slice the buns in half and place on a baking sheet. Spread the inside of each of the buns with Taken Butter, and sprinkle with garlic powder. Place under the broiler, and toast until the buns have slightly browned around the edges.

5. Spread the top of the bun with mayonnaise. Generously spread the bottom of the bun with pâté. Place the cucumber, jalapeños, and cilantro on the bottom bun, and top with the pork patty. Add Pickled Vegetables (page 23) and the top bun.

TOM KHA GOONG

Difficulty: Medium
Prep time: 30 minutes
Cook time: 40 minutes
Yield: 4 servings
Dietary notes: Shellfish; Dairy-Free

I had a delicious bowl of Tom Kha Goong in the Tower some time ago, so I wanted to include a recipe for it in this book. To my surprise, my research revealed that this dish was prepared in many different ways during the Golden Age. I ended up experimenting with the soup for a full week trying to find my favorite. The harmony of the shrimp and the creaminess in this dish is just perfection.

2 teaspoons canola oil
2-inch piece ginger, peeled and sliced
2 stalks lemongrass
3 cloves garlic, sliced
3 cups Dashi Stock (page 24)
1½ cups coconut milk
1 king oyster mushroom, sliced
6 shiitake mushrooms, sliced
1 pound shrimp, peeled and deveined
2 tablespoons fish sauce
2 tablespoons lime juice
2 teaspoons lime zest
Salt and pepper
Pinch of cayenne pepper
2 cups rice, cooked
3 scallions, sliced
Handful of cilantro
Bean sprouts (optional)
2 limes, quartered

1. Place canola oil, ginger, lemongrass, and garlic in a medium pot over medium-high heat. Cook until it becomes fragrant, about 5 minutes. Add Dashi Stock. Bring to a simmer for 20 minutes.

2. Remove the ginger, lemongrass, and garlic. Add the coconut milk, and stir well.

3. Add the mushrooms. Cook until the mushrooms soften, about 5 minutes. Add shrimp, and cook until they turn pink, about 5 minutes. Finally, add the fish sauce, lime juice, and lime zest. Season with salt, pepper, and cayenne pepper to taste.

4. To serve, place cooked rice in a bowl. Pour the soup on top. Garnish with scallions, cilantro, bean sprouts, and lime quarters.

BULGOGI BURRITOS

- ⬛ **Difficulty: Medium**
- 🕐 **Prep time: 12 to 17 hours**
- 🔥 **Cook time: 30 minutes**
- ⚠️ **Yield: 6 servings**
- ⬛ **Dietary notes: Dairy-Free**

The citizens of the Last City have always lived a life of uncertainty and adversity, but the common goal of a better future has brought all kinds of people together. I love recipes that highlight the strengths of the cultures we've lost, but I wanted a dish to celebrate the Guardians and the citizens who work together every day. These burritos, with their delightful mix of spices, celebrate their collaboration in every bite.

Bulgogi Beef.

6 cloves garlic

1 Korean pear, peeled, cored, and chopped

2 pounds skirt steak

½ cup soy sauce

¼ cup white sugar

¼ cup brown sugar

2 tablespoons sesame oil

¼ cup mirin

2 scallions, chopped

3 tablespoons chili powder

1 tablespoon pepper

2 tablespoons canola oil

Rice:

1½ cups rice

1 cup water

2 cups chicken stock

¼ cup cilantro, chopped

Zest and juice of 2 limes

2 teaspoons rice vinegar

1 teaspoon salt

1 tablespoon Shichimi Togarashi (page 20)

3 tablespoons black sesame seeds

Accompaniments:

Large flour tortillas, warmed

Gochujang Tomatillo Salsa (page 22)

Kimchi, cut into bite-size pieces

For the bulgogi beef:

1. Place the garlic and Korean pear in a food processor, and grind until smooth.

2. Transfer into a gallon-size sealable bag with the steak and the next 8 ingredients. Seal the bag, toss to completely coat the meat, and place in the refrigerator overnight, up to 16 hours.

3. Place a medium stainless-steel pan, with 2 tablespoons of canola oil, over high heat. Sear the steak to your desired temperature. Transfer to a plate and cover in aluminum foil. Allow the meat to rest for 10 minutes.

4. Slice the meat against the grain in order to avoid the pieces being chewy. Next, slice into cubes. Cover until you are ready to assemble the burritos.

For the rice:

5. Place the rice, water, and chicken stock in a rice cooker. Follow the instructions on your rice cooker, and cook the rice.

6. Transfer the cooked rice into a non-metal bowl. Mix the cilantro, lime juice, lime zest, rice vinegar, salt, Shichimi Togarashi, and black sesame seeds with the rice. Set aside and keep warm until you are ready to assemble the burritos.

For assembly:

7. Take a large flour tortilla and place between ¼ to ½ cup of cilantro rice in the center. Top with a helping of Gochujang Tomatillo Salsa, kimchi, and beef. Carefully wrap the burrito shut.

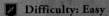

IZANAGI'S BURDEN

One late starry evening, I was walking home from a planning meeting when I stopped by a bar for a quick drink. There I noticed an Exo sitting with an untouched drink in front of her and a cold demeanor. Her armor was covered in a beautifully intricate pattern with several odd symbols on her breastplate. In all of my travels and research, I've seen the symbol only once, referencing something called the "Black Armory." Unfortunately, she wasn't interested in a conversation and left with her sake mojito still untouched. I do wonder from time to time who she was.

½ cup sake
1-inch piece ginger, sliced
1 small cucumber, sliced
3 sprigs fresh cilantro, plus additional
   leaves for garnish
2 tablespoons lime juice
½ cup ginger beer
Ice
Lime slices

1. Combine the sake, ginger, cucumber, and cilantro sprigs in an airtight container. Place in the refrigerator for at least 6 hours, up to 3 days.

2. Fill 2 glasses with ice. Split the flavored sake between the two glasses. Add the lime juice and ginger beer to each. Lightly mix to combine. Garnish with lime slices and additional cilantro leaves.

CAYDE-6

Whenever I used to go out to eat with Cayde, he only ever wanted to dine at the ramen shop. And once there he would always order the Spicy Ramen. One time I tried to convince him to order the Gyudon instead, but he refused, saying he needed "a classy order for a classy Exo." At least the two of us could always agree on getting extra dumplings. I tried to explain to Cayde on more than one occasion how many farms in the area are required to supply enough food for the Tower's population. I figured he should experience all of the foods we're lucky enough to have access to, but I don't think my point ever stuck. The Gyudon recipe in this collection was my attempt to get him to try something new, but I never got the chance show him.

We all miss Cayde. In particular, I worry about Banshee-44. He's such a kind soul, though he sometimes gets so lost in his words that he forgets what he was looking for. But Cayde . . . he never forgets about Cayde.

On occasion I'll make a meal of Gyoza, Spicy Ramen, Gyudon, and Ajitsuke Tamago by which to remember my dear friend. Of course, there's nothing like finishing the meal off with a bright green Ace of Spades drink before getting back to business. Cayde-6 would have wanted us to do it for the Tower, and for the ramen shops. And for the loot.

THE CRUCIBLE

Nothing beats a nice relaxing afternoon, a cup of tea, and some delightful little snacks, but even I find myself cheering on the Guardians in the Crucible from time to time. I try to stop by whenever I hear Ramos is competing to send him some extra good luck. It's so exciting to see Guardians throwing around hammers made of pure fire, dodging bullets like they're nothing, and rising into the air with electricity crackling around them. Why, I don't know if I'd believe it if I didn't see it for myself. I'm happy Shaxx has kept the tradition going for so long and with such passion. He knows how to put on a good show.

There are some Guardian fights I tend to avoid, though. I don't know if you've ever run into the Drifter but listen to old Eva: He's nothing but trouble. I don't know why so many Guardians seek his audience these days, but I stay away as much as possible. The Crucible is where Guardians belong, seeking glory and putting on their best efforts, not in some dingy spaceship.

With all the heroics going on, I had to look back to the Golden Age for some inspirational meals. I've read many a tale of ancient coliseums filled with warriors proving their worth even when there weren't wars to be fought. It gives me such hope for our future that I've put together a few hearty recipes to go along with the triumphs. I even borrowed a few ideas from the concessions sold during the matches. But don't tell Shaxx—I don't think he'd like the competition. Oh, who am I kidding, that fellow lives for it!

ENERGY BARS

⚔ Difficulty: Easy

🕐 Prep time: 1 hour

🕐 Rest time: 4 hours

⚠ Yield: about 50

▨ Dietary notes: Vegan; Tree Nuts

I made these bars for Shaxx to show my gratitude for everything he did for us during the Red War, and he thanked me boisterously with that booming voice you can always hear from across the Tower. These energy bars are exactly what a Guardian needs to keep up their spirit during matches in the Crucible.

2 cups whole cashews

½ cup sunflower seeds

¼ cup pistachios

½ cup white sesame seeds

3 tablespoons chia seeds

2 tablespoons ground flaxseeds

1 cup cashew butter

¼ cup almond butter

¾ cup dried cranberries

⅓ cup dried apricots

2 teaspoons salt

2 teaspoons ground cinnamon

1. Place the cashews, sunflower seeds, and pistachios in a food processor. Pulse until the nuts are completely crumbled. Add the rest of the ingredients, and blend until completely combined.

2. Line a 9-by-9-inch deep baking sheet with parchment paper. Spread the mixture into the baking sheet, and flatten. Place in the refrigerator, and allow to rest for 4 hours. Remove from the baking sheet, and cut into 1½-by-1-inch pieces. These bars can be stored in an airtight container in the refrigerator for up to 2 weeks.

DUCK POUTINE

This incredibly rich poutine recipe uses duck, a creature found far out in the decimated hills near small villages. Though finding these animals can be difficult, a good huntsman can track them down for this savory meal that makes good use of the entire bird.

Duck:

1 whole duck
1 tablespoon Orange and Lime
   Rosemary Salt (page 19)
1 small orange, quartered
3 star anise
1 cinnamon stick

Gravy:

3 tablespoons canola oil, divided
2 pounds chicken wings
1 carrot, roughly chopped
1 celery stalk, roughly chopped
2 shallots, roughly chopped
5 cups Chicken Broth (page 25)
1 duck carcass
1 tablespoon dried sage
3 dried bay leaves
4 dried shiitake mushrooms
2 tablespoons whole
   black peppercorns
¼ cup duck fat
½ cup flour
Salt and pepper

For the duck:

1. Preheat oven to 300°F. Prepare a baking sheet with aluminum foil, and then top with a wire rack. Rub the duck with the Orange and Lime Rosemary Salt. Place the duck, breast side up, on the wire rack. Stuff the cavity with the quartered oranges, star anise, and cinnamon stick. Roast for 2 hours, or until the breast is cooked.

2. Break down the duck. Place the meat in an airtight container, and set the carcass aside. Allow the meat to cool completely and store in the refrigerator until you are ready to serve it.

For the gravy:

3. Place a pot over medium-high heat with 1 tablespoon of the canola oil. Add and brown the chicken wings. Transfer to a plate once browned.

4. Add the remaining canola oil. Add the carrots, celery, and shallots. Cook until slightly softened, about 5 minutes. Add the Chicken Broth. Add the chicken wings, duck carcass, sage, bay leaves, dried shiitake mushrooms, and whole black peppercorns.

5. Bring the mixture to a boil, and then reduce the heat to medium-low. Keep the broth at a simmer, uncovered, for at least 3½ hours. Season with salt and pepper to taste. Once the broth is ready, strain and set the broth aside. The broth can be stored in the refrigerator for up to 3 days.

6. Place a pot over medium-high heat. Melt the duck fat in the pot. Once the fat has melted, whisk in the flour. Slowly add the broth while whisking. It is very important that you do this slowly and to be constantly whisking. This will allow the gravy to become nice and thick. Bring to a boil, and then reduce the heat. Simmer until the gravy has thickened. Season with salt and pepper to taste.

* Continued on page 99

Potato Wedges:

¼ cup duck fat, melted

2 teaspoons garlic powder

1 teaspoon ground ginger

2 teaspoons dried rosemary

Pinch of cayenne pepper

1 teaspoon pepper

2 teaspoons salt

3 russet potatoes, cut into wedges
  or thick fries

Toppings:

12 ounces cheese curds

2 green onions, diced

For the potato wedges:

7. Preheat oven to 450°F. Combine the duck fat, garlic powder, ground ginger, rosemary, cayenne pepper, pepper, and salt in a large bowl. Add and toss the potato wedges.

8. Prepare a baking sheet with aluminum foil and nonstick spray. Transfer the seasoned potato wedges onto the sheet. Place in the oven, and bake for 15 minutes. Toss and bake for another 15 minutes. Toss once more, and bake for another 10 minutes. Turn on the broiler and cook the fries until they are crispy, about 4 to 5 minutes.

For the toppings:

9. In a bowl, place a large portion of fries. Top with cheese curds, green onion, and shredded duck. Add a few scoops of gravy on top.

BEEF STEW

Difficulty: Medium
Prep time: 1 hour
Cook time: 4 hours
Yield: 6 servings
Dietary notes: None

I sometimes make this beef stew for a few friends of mine who compete in the Crucible. It's got a great heartiness to get you back on your feet after spending an afternoon facing down your peers again and again. Even if a competitor has had bad luck in their matches, this meal will rejuvenate their spirits, helping them get back into the arena and continue to hone their skills in order to be ready for the next battle to defend the City.

2 tablespoons salt

1 tablespoon pepper

1 tablespoon ground sage

3 pounds boneless beef short ribs, cut into 1-inch cubes

5 tablespoons canola oil, divided

¼ cup flour

4 carrots, peeled and cut into 1-inch medallions

3 celery stalks, cut into 1-inch pieces

2 yellow onions, sliced

1 cup dry red wine

¼ cup tomato paste

4 cups beef broth

3 dried bay leaves

8 ounces white pearl onions, skin removed

8 ounces red pearl onions, skin removed

2 tablespoons unsalted butter

¼ cup plus 3 tablespoons water, divided

5 ounces baby portobello mushrooms, quartered

10 ounces button mushrooms, quartered

2 tablespoons cornstarch

16 ounces egg noodles, cooked

1. Preheat oven to 325°F. Combine salt, pepper, and sage in a small bowl, then use to season the beef short ribs.

2. Place a Dutch oven over medium heat, and add 1 tablespoon of the canola oil. Add a single layer of the beef, being careful not to overcrowd the Dutch oven. Brown all sides of the meat. Remove and place on a plate. Add additional canola oil, if needed, and continue this process until all the beef has been browned. Toss the browned beef with flour.

3. Add another tablespoon of canola oil to the Dutch oven. Add carrots, celery, and onions, and cook until the onions soften, about 5 minutes.

4. Add the beef back to the Dutch oven, and stir together. Mix in the red wine, tomato paste, and beef broth. Stir until the tomato paste has incorporated with the rest of the liquid. Add bay leaves, and cover with a lid. Place in the oven, and cook for 3 hours, or until the beef is tender.

5. About 30 minutes before the stew is done, place a pan over medium-high heat. Add 2 teaspoons of canola oil and cook the pearl onions until they start to brown. Add the butter and cook until the butter melts. Add ¼ cup of water and cover. Reduce the heat to medium, and allow the onions to soften (but do not allow them to become mushy and lose their shape), about 15 minutes. Remove any remaining liquid, and set aside until the stew is ready.

6. In another pan, over medium-high heat, cook the mushrooms until browned. Set aside until the stew is ready.

7. Once the stew has finished cooking, carefully pour the contents of the Dutch oven through a mesh strainer with a bowl underneath to collect the liquid. Return the beef and vegetables to the Dutch oven.

8. Place the liquid in a 2-quart saucepan, and cook over medium heat. In a small bowl, combine cornstarch and remaining water. Once the liquid is simmering, whisk in the cornstarch slurry, and mix until sauce thickens.

9. Pour the thickened sauce back to the Dutch oven. Add the pearl onions and mushrooms. Stir the contents together. Serve over a bowl of egg noodles.

PORK TENDERLOIN

Difficulty: Easy
Prep time: 1 hour
Cook time: 1 hour
Yield: 4 servings
Dietary notes: Dairy-Free

I approached Saladin the last time he was in town to propose a city-wide celebration of the Iron Banner, but he considers the event to be more about duty than merriment. Although I understand where he's coming from, with all that he's seen as one of the last Iron Lords, I still couldn't help but make a special dish to commemorate the holiday.

2 pounds red potatoes, peeled and cut into 1-inch portions

¼ cup olive oil

2 tablespoons balsamic vinegar

1 tablespoon honey

8 ounces brussels sprouts, stemmed and cut in half

½ red onion, cut into ¼-by-½-inch rectangles

Salt and pepper

2½ tablespoons Orange and Lime Rosemary Salt (page 19)

2 teaspoons Shichimi Togarashi (page 20)

20 cloves garlic, minced

2 pounds pork tenderloin, split into 2 portions

1. Preheat oven to 425°F. Cook red potatoes in a pot of boiling water for 8 minutes. Strain and set aside. Combine olive oil, balsamic vinegar, and honey in a large bowl. Toss in potatoes, brussels sprouts, and red onions to coat. Season with salt and pepper to taste. Set aside.

2. Combine Orange and Lime Rosemary Salt, Shichimi Togarashi, and garlic together in a small bowl. Rub each of the pork tenderloins. Place in the center of a baking sheet. Place the vegetables around the pork tenderloin. Roast for 30 to 45 minutes, or until the pork registers an internal temperature of 145°F. Set the broiler to high, and cook until the pork crisps, about 4 minutes. Remove from the oven, cover in aluminum foil, and allow to rest for 10 minutes before slicing.

WHOLE CHICKEN

⚔ Difficulty: Easy

🕐 Prep time: 6 to 13 hours

🔥 Cook time: 1½ to 2 hours

⚠ Yield: 8 servings

⬡ Dietary notes: Dairy-Free

When I was away from the Tower, I started missing the spectacle of the Crucible. The Farm had an old field where people would kick a ball around, but of course it couldn't approach the scale and excitement of the arena. While I had access to the plentiful chickens running around out there, I started developing this recipe. Since I returned to the City, I've perfected the dish, which has found a huge following among Crucible combatants, who love the delicious flavor and all the protein it has to offer.

Brined Chicken:

2 quarts water

⅓ cup lemon juice

⅓ cup salt

¼ cup sugar

2 tablespoons black peppercorns

4 sprigs fresh rosemary

2 lemons, sliced

2 cups ice

2 whole chickens, each about 5 pounds

4 dried bay leaves

Spice Rub:

¼ cup Lemon Garlic Pepper Salt (page 18)

1½ tablespoons Orange and Lime Rosemary Salt (page 19)

2 tablespoons dried tarragon

Roast Chicken:

2 lemons, cut in half

8 cloves garlic

For the brined chicken:

1. Combine water, lemon juice, salt, sugar, peppercorns, rosemary, and sliced lemons in a large pot. Place over medium-high heat until the salt dissolves. Remove from the heat, and add ice cubes. Allow to cool completely.

2. Place each chicken in a sealable bag with 2 bay leaves in each. Divide the cooled brine (including everything) between the bags. Place in the refrigerator and allow to marinate for at least 5 hours, up to 12 hours.

For the spice rub:

3. Preheat oven to 375°F. Remove the chickens from the refrigerator and sealable bags (reserve the rosemary). Pat dry, and place in a large baking dish. Combine the ingredients of the spice rub in a small bowl. Rub each chicken thoroughly, inside and out.

For the roast chicken:

4. Insert the lemon, rosemary (from the brine), and garlic in the cavity of each chicken. Bake, breast side up, for 1½ to 2 hours, or until the chicken registers an internal temperature of 165°F. Remove from the oven, and cover with aluminum foil. Let rest for 10 minutes before carving.

SMOKED TURKEY LEGS

⚔ **Difficulty: Hard**

🕐 **Prep time: 24 hours**

🔥 **Cook time: 2 to 3 hours**

⚠ **Yield: 6 servings**

⛏ **Dietary notes: Dairy-Free**

When Saladin takes over the arenas and brings forth the thrill that is the Iron Banner, the concession stands serve these turkey legs for all the cheering spectators. I always have eyes larger than my stomach and have never managed to finish one by myself, but I'll never pass up an opportunity to order one. I got this recipe straight from the vendor. While making these is a time-consuming process, the deep flavor certainly makes the wait worth it!

Turkey Brine:
8 cups water

½ cup salt

¼ cup Lemon Garlic Pepper Salt (page 18)

2 tablespoons Spicy Smoked Paprika Salt (page 18)

½ cup brown sugar

¼ cup white sugar

2 cups ice

6 turkey legs

4 dried bay leaves

Dry Rub:
2 tablespoons chili powder

1 tablespoon cumin

1 tablespoon Lemon Garlic Pepper Salt (page 18)

½ tablespoon Spicy Smoked Paprika Salt (page 18)

2 teaspoons brown sugar

Extra Equipment:
Wood chips

Charcoal briquettes

For the turkey brine:

1. Combine the water, salt, Lemon Garlic Pepper Salt, Spicy Smoked Paprika Salt, brown sugar, and white sugar in a pot. Place over medium-high heat until the salt dissolves. Remove from heat, and add ice cubes to allow it to cool completely.

2. Split the turkey legs in 2 sealable bags with 2 bay leaves in each. Divide the cooled, spiced brine between the bags. Place in the refrigerator, and allow to marinate for at least 24 hours, up to 48 hours.

3. Place 4 large handfuls of wood chips in water, and let soak for at least 1 hour. Before setting up your smoking station, remove the turkey legs out of the brine (do not throw out the brine), and pat dry.

For the dry rub:

4. Mix together the spices for the dry rub in a bowl. Rub the spices on the turkey legs, and set aside until your grill is ready.

5. Using a charcoal grill, light charcoal briquettes in a chimney starter. Once the charcoal turns slightly white, toss it out of the chimney to one side of the grill. On the other side, place a disposable, deep aluminum pan, and fill halfway with the reserved brine.

6. Making sure to remove as much water as possible, add a handful of wood chips to the top of the charcoal. Place the grill rack, and cover the grill. Let the grill heat up; the temperature should be 250° to 340°F, though using the lower temperature is recommended.

7. Place the turkey legs on the side of the grill over the aluminum pan. Add more wood and charcoal as needed throughout the cooking time. Cook for 2 to 3 hours, or until the turkey registers at 165°F on a thermometer.

TWICE-BAKED SWEET POTATOES

- Difficulty: Medium
- Prep time: 45 minutes
- Cook time: 1½ hours
- Yield: 4 servings
- Dietary notes: Dairy

I saw a few Crucible contestants enjoying a plate of something with a side of what looked like sweet potatoes. Suddenly, one of them shouted in excitement about some sweet business they finally found. I have to assume they were talking about the sweet potatoes they were eating, so this dish must be a hit at arenas. The contestants were just so excited that I had to include my own sweet potato recipe in this book.

4 medium sweet potatoes,
  scrubbed clean
Olive oil
Salt
Canola oil
3 shallots, thinly sliced
¼ cup chopped chives
6 slices bacon, cooked and chopped
2 tablespoons unsalted butter
2 fresh sage leaves
¼ cup coconut cream
2 teaspoons Spicy Smoked Paprika
  Salt (page 18)
Honey

1. Preheat oven to 425°F. Poke several holes into the sweet potatoes with a fork. Rub each with olive oil and season with salt. Bake for 1 hour, or until soft and cooked through. Once cooked, set aside until cool enough to work with. Reduce the oven to 350°F.

2. Place a pan with canola oil over medium-low heat. Add the shallots and sprinkle with salt. Sauté until softened and slightly caramelized, about 5 minutes. Remove from heat, and set aside. Mix in a bowl with chives and cooked bacon.

3. When the potatoes are cool enough to handle, cut them in half lengthwise. Scoop the inside into a bowl while leaving about ¼ inch thick wall in the potato.

4. Place the butter, sage leaves, and coconut cream in a pot over medium heat. Allow the butter to melt. Let the sage cook in the butter for 3 minutes, and then remove. Add the sweet potato interior and mash until smooth. Turn off heat. Add the Spicy Smoked Paprika Salt. Season with additional salt and pepper if needed.

5. Place the mashed potatoes in each of the potato skins. Top with shallots, chives, and bacon. Bake for 15 minutes. Turn on the broiler and cook until crispy. Drizzle with honey.

Difficulty: Easy
Prep time: 15 minutes
Cook time: 15 minutes
Yield: 4 servings
Dietary notes: Vegan

THORN

I came up with this recipe a few weeks ago, after digging through some Golden Age engrams, and the results were just splendid. I've named it after speaking to Shaxx, who told me that he was dealing with some business with "thorns." I figured it was a perfect name for this particular drink.

6 whole cloves
2 cinnamon sticks
4 star anise
½ cup brown sugar
1½ cups apple cider
One 750-ml bottle dry red wine
1 orange, sliced
1 grapefruit, sliced

1. Place the cloves, cinnamon sticks, and star anise in a cheesecloth. Wrap it up and tie it closed with butcher's twine.

2. In a pot, mix the brown sugar and apple cider. Add the spice bundle, wine, and sliced fruit into the pot. Bring to a low simmer. Simmer for 15 minutes. Serve hot, garnished with extra spices if desired.

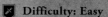

🗡 **Difficulty: Easy**
🕐 **Prep time: 10 minutes**
⚠ **Yield: 3 servings**
▨ **Dietary notes: Dairy**

COLDHEART

When I was watching a Crucible match the other day, I saw a weapon that was emitting a beautiful ray of light. A fellow spectator told me that it's called Coldheart and has the tendency to freeze the hands of those who use it. I was fascinated by that eerie glow and wanted to record it for posterity, so I pulled out a notepad and came up with the concept for this drink on the spot—though I hope it doesn't injure anyone's hands when they enjoy it.

1 banana, peeled
3 kiwis, peeled
1 avocado, peeled and pitted
1 cup frozen mango
1 cup fresh spinach
2 mint leaves
½ cup Greek yogurt
1 cup coconut milk
Juice of 1 lemon

1. Combine everything in a blender, and blend until smooth.

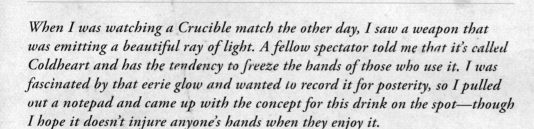

EDZ: THE FARM

The Farm, as the Guardians like to call it, is one of many outposts that supply the Last City with the resources it needs to keep going. Not only that, but it was also home for me for quite some time. I was injured during the Red War, but thanks to the help of a few brave souls I made my way to the Farm to recuperate. At the time, I honestly didn't plan on ever coming back to the Tower. Sometimes it's nice to be grounded on earth instead of metal and concrete. But I couldn't stay away for long after hearing from Tess that the Tower holidays were being planned and run without me. I had put so much effort into the Dawning, the Festival of the Lost, and the rest. There was no way I was going to let someone usurp my responsibilities!

Although Suraya Hawthorne was often out on scouting missions or working with other Guardians, I got to spend a lot of time with her and Louis during my stay at the Farm. I must say, Suraya reminds me a lot of myself when I was younger. She's fierce and independent, and she doesn't let others do her work for her. We often spoke in the evenings when she had the time, discussing what the future held and what we could do to help the others. At the time, the Tower was still lost and the Last City a war zone. Suraya isn't the kind to be content behind walls, but she cared for the people who were displaced.

As soon as I recovered, I tried to make myself less of a burden. Old Eva wasn't going to be lounging around all day! Fortunately, I had a few notes from some Golden Age entries on camping, and I quickly found a few helpful snacks that the scouting parties could take with them: dried goods, easily packaged meals, and even a little birdseed as a thank-you to Louis. I hope you'll give them a try! When you're feeling cooped up in the Last City, make yourself some s'mores and it'll seem like you're exploring the outdoors again.

ELIKSNI BIRDSEED

Difficulty: Easy

Prep time: 10 minutes

Yield: 8 servings

Dietary notes: Dairy; Tree Nuts; Vegetarian

A gorgeous falcon and wonderful protector, Louis has been keeping watch for Hawthorne since before the Red War. He was also lovely company when I was on the Farm, so I came up with a recipe that both of us could enjoy. I add the chocolate just for my portion—please be sure to leave that out when making this for feathered companions.

¾ cup whole roasted and
   salted cashews

¾ cup dark chocolate–covered
   almonds (for humans only)

½ cup sliced almonds

½ cup dark chocolate chips
   (for humans only)

1 cup walnuts

½ cup sunflower seeds, hulled

½ cup roasted pumpkin seeds

1 cup dried cherries

½ cup dried cranberries

1. Mix everything in an airtight container and enjoy.

BEEF JERKY

Difficulty: Easy

Prep time: 12 hours

Cook time: 4 to 5 hours

Yield: 2 pounds of jerky

Dietary notes: Dairy-Free

My jerky recipe has been tested by hungry warriors through long battles, overnight patrols, and extended voyages. I've collected feedback from the strong and the weak, the bravest and the hungriest. Trust me, dear, nothing is more satisfying.

1 Korean pear, peeled, cored,
   and chopped
½ cup soy sauce
¼ cup honey
¼ cup brown sugar
2 tablespoons sesame oil
2 tablespoons mirin
1 tablespoon garlic paste
2 tablespoons ginger paste
3 tablespoons gochujang
1 tablespoon pepper
2 pounds top round beef roast,
   thinly sliced

1. Puree the Korean pear in a food processor until smooth. Combine the pureed Korean pear, soy sauce, honey, brown sugar, sesame oil, mirin, garlic paste, ginger paste, gochujang, and pepper in a gallon-size sealable bag. Add the thinly sliced beef, seal, and shake until the beef is covered in the marinade. Place in the refrigerator overnight, up to 18 hours.

2. Preheat oven to 175°F. Prepare a baking sheet by covering it in aluminum foil, placing a wire rack on top, and spraying the rack with nonstick spray. Take the beef out of the marinade, and let excess liquid drip off. Place on the wire rack.

3. Bake for 4 to 5 hours, or until the beef is dry and chewy. Let cool completely. The jerky can be stored in an airtight container in the refrigerator for up to 1 week.

SPLIT PEA SOUP

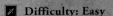

⚔ **Difficulty: Easy**
🕐 **Prep time: 30 minutes**
🔥 **Cook time: 1½ hours**
⛺ **Yield: 5 servings**
🏔 **Dietary notes: Dairy**

Suraya Hawthorne always had a soft spot for newcomers to the Farm, who stumbled in from the chaos of the world outside—just as she did all those years ago. This is one of her favorite recipes to prepare for new refugees, guaranteed to warm the stomach and the spirit. Don't be afraid to experiment with the seasoning. As you know, Suraya has never been one for following rules. She'd never prescribe you just one unchangeable split pea soup recipe, just as she'd never tell you what path to walk in life. We can all learn from her in that regard.

2 tablespoons unsalted butter

1 tablespoon olive oil

4 shallots, chopped

1 medium carrot, peeled and chopped

1 celery stalk, chopped

Salt and pepper

1 pound ham, cut into cubes

2 smoked ham hocks

1 quart Chicken Broth (page 25)

2 cups water

16 ounces dry split peas

2 dried bay leaves

3 fresh thyme sprigs

Goat cheese, for garnish

Chives, for garnish

1. In a large stockpot, melt the butter and olive oil over medium heat. Add the shallots, carrot, and celery. Season with salt and pepper to taste. Cook until vegetables become soft, 10 to 15 minutes. Add the cubed ham and cook until lightly browned, 3 to 5 minutes.

2. Add the ham hocks, Chicken Broth, water, split peas, bay leaves, and thyme sprigs. Cover, bring to a simmer, then reduce heat so it doesn't boil, and cook for 1½ to 2 hours or until the split peas are falling apart and the soup thickens.

3. Remove the ham hocks, bay leaves, and thyme sprigs. Season with salt and pepper to taste again, if needed. Serve with a dollop of goat cheese and a few chive stalks.

TINFOIL SNAPPER

⚔ **Difficulty:** Easy

🕐 **Prep time:** 15 minutes

🔥 **Cook time:** 45 minutes

⚠ **Yield:** 1 whole fish

⛰ **Dietary notes:**
Dairy-Free

This old recipe of mine reminds me of Cayde-6. Once I was planning on cooking some snapper but couldn't find my tinfoil. After asking around, I found out that a Guardian had taken it to create his version of something called a Spinfoil Hat, which was something he heard Cayde-6 had possessed. I don't know why he didn't just ask me for some, as I would have been happy to lend it to him if he had only asked first. Please remember this on your travels, my friend: Never feel shame in asking for help. Because when you do, you'll often find that you've gained not just the items you needed but also a new friend.

2 teaspoons Lemon Garlic Pepper
   Salt (page 18)

½ teaspoon cayenne pepper

1 teaspoon ground coriander

1 whole snapper, fins, scales, and
   guts removed

1 lemon, sliced

1 orange, sliced

3 fresh rosemary sprigs

Olive oil, for drizzling

1. Preheat oven to 350°F. Combine the Lemon Garlic Pepper Salt, cayenne pepper, and ground coriander in a small bowl. Rub all parts of the snapper with the spice mixture.

2. Take a large sheet of aluminum foil and place half of the lemon and orange slices in the center. Place the seasoned snapper on top. Stuff the cavity of the snapper with the rosemary sprigs. Top with the remaining lemon and orange slices. Drizzle with olive oil. Loosely seal the aluminum together, enclosing the snapper.

3. Place in the oven, and bake for 30 minutes. Open up the sealed pack and increase the oven temperature to 425°F. Bake for another 10 minutes, or until the fish is flaky.

TOMATO AND ROASTED GARLIC FOCACCIA

Difficulty: Easy
Prep time: 2 hours
Cook time: 20 minutes
Yield: 1 loaf
Dietary notes: Vegan

This focaccia bread is the perfect dish to share with others. Out on the Farm, it was something I encouraged Hawthorne to share with Devrim, as it's deceptively simple but full of flavor and goes great with a cup of tea—and we all know how Devrim loves a good cuppa.

2¼ teaspoons active dry yeast

2 teaspoons sugar

1 tablespoon salt

3 tablespoons olive oil, plus more
   for brushing dough

1⅓ cup lukewarm water

4 cups all-purpose flour

Sea salt flakes

15 cherry tomatoes, cut in half

20 cloves garlic, roasted and
   roughly chopped

1. Combine the yeast, sugar, salt, 3 tablespoons of the olive oil, and water in a bowl. Let rest for 5 minutes, or until the yeast becomes active. Add the flour, and mix until it just comes together. Transfer to a lightly floured surface, and knead for 5 minutes. Shape into a ball.

2. Brush a bowl with an even coating of olive oil and place the dough in it. Brush the top of the dough with additional olive oil. Cover, and let the dough rise until it has doubled in size, about 1 hour.

3. Prepare a 15-by-10-inch baking sheet by brushing it with olive oil and then sprinkling with sea salt flakes. Transfer the dough directly onto the baking sheet. Carefully spread the dough until it completely covers the baking sheet. If the dough seems to be too resistant to spreading, cover and let rest for 10 minutes, and then continue stretching it out.

4. Once the dough is spread in the baking sheet, cover and let rest for 15 minutes. Using your fingers, poke several deep wells throughout the dough. Lightly brush with olive oil. Add the cherry tomatoes and garlic by pushing them into the wells you created in the dough. Cover again, and let rest for 40 minutes.

5. Preheat oven to 425°F. Uncover the dough, and top with sea salt flakes. Bake for 18 to 20 minutes, or until the top is golden brown. Remove from the oven and top with additional sea salt flakes. Let cool completely before cutting into pieces.

S'MORES BARK

- Difficulty: Easy
- Prep time: 20 minutes
- Cook time: 10 minutes
- Yield: 16 to 20 s'mores
- Dietary notes: Dairy

While these goodies are baking, they will fill your home with delicious smells. Their decadent sweetness will put a smile on everyone's faces—Warlock, Hunter, Titan, and civilian alike.

5 graham cracker sheets

18 ounces dark chocolate

6 ounces white chocolate

1 cup Marshmallows, cut into small pieces (page 27 or packaged)

½ cup chocolate chips

Sea salt flakes, for topping

1. Line a 10-by-10-inch baking sheet with parchment paper. Lightly crumble three of the graham crackers, and spread them evenly on the baking sheet. Microwave the dark chocolate in a medium-size bowl, stirring every 30 seconds until fully melted. Pour the chocolate on top of the graham crackers in an even layer.

2. Microwave the white chocolate in a small bowl, stirring every 30 seconds until fully melted. Pour the white chocolate on top of the dark chocolate, and swirl together with a toothpick.

3. Preheat oven broiler. Crumble the remaining two graham crackers, and sprinkle over the chocolate. Top with Marshmallows and chocolate chips. Press topping down lightly to fuse with the chocolate. Broil for 1 to 2 minutes, or until the Marshmallows are golden.

4. Allow to cool, and place in the refrigerator for 1 hour. Top with a generous sprinkle of sea salt flakes. Cut into small portions. Transfer to an airtight container, and store at room temperature for up to 1 week.

DEVRIM KAY AND SURAYA HAWTHORNE

You already know that I think Devrim Kay is a true gentleman and it's common knowledge that he loves his tea. When I was at the Farm, Devrim came by on occasion to check in, and whenever we got together for tea, I found him to be kind and sincere. We don't agree on everything, though: He thought I should defend myself by picking up weapons and doing battle, but I know that is not my lot in life. I have faith that the Guardians will defend us, no matter what new challenge comes our way. During my time at the Farm, I never intended to go back to the City. I found myself useful on the Farm, cooking up a variety of dishes with direct access to a variety of fresh ingredients.

Hawthorne has told me how strange it feels to be holed up in the Tower while Devrim is posted out in the wild. "Feels a bit backward, you know?" she said to me once. "I'm the one who left, not him."

Devrim does fret over Hawthorne's frequent check-ins, telling her she must let him focus on his work. But I'm sure he'll hush his complaints if she brings him snacks like my Eliksni Birdseed and Beef Jerky, as well as some tea. We know he would drink tea with anything.

It's been a real joy watching Hawthorne grow up into a strong, courageous leader. I'm impressed with how well she handles impulsive Guardians and organizes their clans now, considering she didn't trust them back on the Farm. She's even been known to sit down for S'mores Bark with the Guardians when the day's work is done. Nothing will ever break the strong connection between Hawthorne and Devrim, but I hope that one day soon they will sit down and share a meal together, either at the Farm or in the Tower.

EDZ: TROSTLAND

Sometimes I wish I had the opportunity to venture out of the Last City and explore the ruins and echoes of the Golden Age in person. Perhaps if I were a few years younger, I could join Devrim on his scouting missions and see firsthand what has been left behind by centuries of decay. I've considered asking a few Guardian friends of mine to take me on a history expedition, but they are all far too busy for a sightseeing trip. If I ever get the chance, I'd love to visit Devrim's outpost and see the ruins of Trostland for myself.

The area where Devrim is stationed used to be the center of a beautiful Western European town named Trostland that bustled with activity during the Golden Age. Now it's a pillaged monument to what once was, plagued with the Fallen scavenging for anything of material value. But they wouldn't know something of value if it hit them on the side of their terrible-looking heads! Devrim trades in weapons and other valuables in exchange for trinkets and other information that Guardians in the area happen upon. He has managed to amass an entire archive of artifacts and engrams that reveal what life was like before everything stopped.

The entries on Trostland paint a beautiful picture I wish I could re-create, so I'm doing my part to restore what I can. Using my research in the Tower archives and some help from Devrim, I've created a set of recipes that helps represent the culinary scene that once existed in the region. I'd love to expand outward and create more snapshots of the past, but the Guardians' presence in Trostland makes this first batch of recipes the perfect testing ground. If you find yourself on a mission and see an engram, be sure to bring it back for archiving!

PRETZELS

⬡ **Difficulty: Hard**

🕐 **Prep time: 2 hours**

🔥 **Cook time: 20 minutes**

⚠ **Yield: 12 servings**

▦ **Dietary notes:
Dairy; Vegetarian**

*The Salt Mines in Trostland are a fantastic—though dangerous—source of
salt. It's very much worth the risk, as a pretzel without salt is a very sad affair!*

Pretzel Dough:

1½ cups all-purpose flour

1½ cups bread flour

2 tablespoons diastatic malt powder

1 cup warm water

2¼ teaspoons active dry yeast

1 tablespoon sugar

1 teaspoon salt

1 tablespoon unsalted butter, melted
  and cooled

Olive oil, for bowl

Egg Wash:

1 egg

1 tablespoon water

Water Bath:

½ cup baking soda

2 quarts water

Accompaniments:

Salt mixtures (page 18 or 19),
  for sprinkling

For pretzel dough:

1. Combine all-purpose flour, bread flour, and malt powder in a medium
bowl. Combine the water, yeast, sugar, and salt in a large bowl. Let rest
for 5 minutes, or until the yeast becomes active. Add the flour mixture
and start to mix together, adding the melted butter before the mixture is
fully combined.

2. Knead for 5 minutes. Transfer to an oiled bowl. Cover, and let the
dough rise until it has doubled in size, about 1 hour.

For the egg wash:

3. Preheat oven to 400°F. Prepare 2 baking sheets with aluminum foil
and nonstick spray. Prepare an egg wash by combining the egg and 1
tablespoon water. Set aside.

For the water bath:

4. Prepare a water bath by combining the baking soda and 2 quarts water
in a large pot. Bring to a boil over medium-high heat. In the meantime,
punch the dough down and split into 12 pieces. Take a portion and roll out
into a thin rope about 20 inches long.

5. To form the pretzel shape, start by making an upside-down "U" shape.
Cross the two ends over each other. Cross the ends one more time. Take
the ends and flip them over the bottom of the "U" and press down. Repeat
with the remaining portions. Allow the dough to rest for 5 minutes.

6. Place the pretzels in the boiling water. Cook for 30 seconds each side.
Use a slotted spoon to take the pretzels out and allow the excess liquid to
drain. Place the pretzels on the prepared baking sheets. Brush with egg
wash. Sprinkle tops with salt mixture of choice. Bake the pretzels for 12 to
15 minutes, or until golden brown.

SCHNITZEL

Difficulty: Medium
Prep time: 30 minutes
Cook time: 30 minutes
Yield: 4 servings
Dietary notes: Dairy-Free; Eggs

The church in the center of Trostland is a favorite spot of Devrim's. Aside from the obvious benefits, like a high vantage point and an excellent place to store his tea, the echoing stone halls make him feel at peace. Perhaps the church reminds him of how things used to be and what they could be again. According to records found in the area, this Schnitzel recipe was a common dish that was made with a variety of meats, though I suppose it was much easier to find a broader variety of livestock during the Golden Age than it is nowadays.

4 boneless pork loin chops
(about 1 pound)
Salt and pepper
⅔ cup all-purpose flour
1 teaspoon garlic powder
2 eggs
1 cup bread crumbs
Peanut oil
1 lemon, sliced

1. Prepare the pork chop by flattening it to ¼-inch thick with a meat tenderizer, and generously season both sides with salt and pepper.

2. Set up 3 stations to bread the pork. On a plate, combine flour and garlic powder. In a bowl, whisk 2 eggs. On another plate, place the bread crumbs.

3. Take a pork chop, and cover it in the flour mixture first. Dip into the eggs, and make sure the chop is fully coated, then let the excess drip off. Finally, coat with the bread crumbs. Set aside, and repeat for remaining portions.

4. Place a ½ inch of peanut oil in a large, deep pan. Heat the oil to about 325°F. Carefully fry the pork for 2 minutes on each side. Transfer to a plate with paper towels to drain. Serve with a slice of lemon.

GERMAN POTATO SALAD

Difficulty: Easy
Prep time: 30 minutes
Cook time: 30 minutes
Yield: 5 servings
Dietary notes: Dairy-Free

Very few things remain intact in Trostland after so many years of ruin, but the Guardians occasionally return with engrams and other bits of information from years long past. Fortunately for me, when they come across anything of cultural value, it gets stored in the Tower library, where I have access to it. This recipe is one such gem.

2 pounds red potatoes, washed and cut into 1-inch pieces

¼ cup white vinegar

1 tablespoon sugar

1 tablespoon Dijon mustard

1 tablespoon lemon juice

½ pound bacon, thinly sliced

3 shallots, sliced

2 tablespoons chives, chopped

Salt and pepper

1. Place potatoes in a pot with cold water and a pinch of salt. Bring the water to a boil over medium-high heat. Reduce heat to medium, and simmer for 10 to 15 minutes, or until potatoes can be easily pierced with a fork. Strain the potatoes, and place in a medium bowl.

2. Combine the white vinegar, sugar, Dijon mustard, and lemon juice. Set aside. Place a large frying pan over medium-high heat, and cook the bacon until crispy. Once cooked, transfer the bacon to a paper-towel-covered plate, but keep about ¼ cup of rendered fat in the pan. Reduce the heat to medium. Add the shallots, and cook until lightly browned, about 5 minutes.

3. Add the vinegar mixture, and increase the heat to medium-high. Cook until it just comes to a boil. Take off the heat, and let sit for 5 minutes.

4. Lightly toss the potatoes with dressing from the pan. Let sit for 5 minutes. Add chives, and toss once more, then season with salt and pepper to taste.

BRAISED RED CABBAGE AND APPLES

⚔ Difficulty: Easy
🕐 Prep time: 30 minutes
🔥 Cook time: 45 minutes
⚠ Yield: 5 servings
✦ Dietary notes: Vegan

I've often had to come up with creative ways to dye cloth and other fabrics, especially when supplies are scarce. I had some extra red cabbage from dying some beautiful red Titan Marks, so I came up with this recipe that also uses other odds and ends I had lying around. Experimenting in the kitchen is such a wonderful example of being open to possibilities in life. Don't forget that red cabbage can stain!

1 tablespoon coconut oil

½ yellow onion, thinly sliced

1 Granny Smith apple, thinly sliced

Salt and pepper

½ medium red cabbage, core removed and thinly sliced

2 tablespoons apple cider vinegar

1 tablespoon rice vinegar

1 tablespoon brown sugar

½ cup water

1. Melt the coconut oil in a large, deep pot over medium-high heat. Add the onions and apple slices, then cook until softened, about 8 minutes. Add a pinch of salt and pepper.

2. Add the sliced cabbage, stir together, and cook for 5 minutes. Add the apple cider vinegar, rice vinegar, brown sugar, and water. Bring to a light boil, and then reduce the heat to medium-low. Cover and cook until the cabbage is tender, about 25 to 30 minutes. Season with additional salt and pepper.

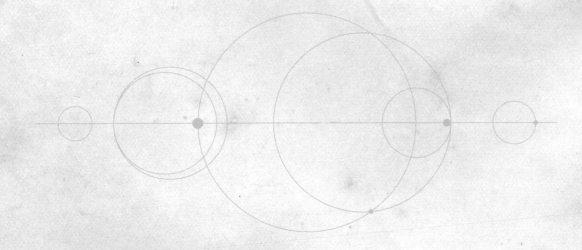

FRENCH ONION SOUP

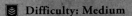
■ Difficulty: Medium
◷ Prep time: 1 hour
◉ Cook time: 2 hours
⚠ Yield: 5 servings
▨ Dietary notes: Dairy

This recipe is a bit of a deviation from the French onion soups I've read about while researching the foods found in the EDZ. I had run out of the stock I typically use in my recipe, so I substituted my Dashi Stock in its place. I thought the replacement was delicious, but when I shared some with Tess, I could tell she felt like the spirit of the recipe was ruined. Tess has a fine taste for food, but sometimes she's too rigid with her preferences. Flexibility, my friend, is the only way to survive—the restraints of our world change constantly, and we will tire ourselves to death if we have to have everything just so.

¼ cup unsalted butter
2½ pounds yellow onions, sliced
1 pound shallots, sliced
2 teaspoons salt
1 teaspoon pepper
2 teaspoons sugar
¼ cup all-purpose flour
½ cup dry white wine
2 quarts Dashi Stock (page 24)
1 roll French bread, ½-inch-thick slices
Olive oil
Gruyère cheese, shredded

1. Place a large stockpot on the stove over medium-low heat. Add the butter and melt, then add the onions and shallots. Cover and cook for 20 minutes.

2. Uncover, and season with salt, pepper, and sugar. Decrease the heat to low, and let the onions and shallots slowly cook for 45 minutes to 1 hour. Stir occasionally, and reduce the heat if the onions are charring before they caramelize.

3. When the onions have caramelized to a deep brown, add the flour, and stir for about 2 minutes. Add the dry white wine, and increase the heat to medium high. Allow the wine to reduce by half. Add the Dashi Stock, and bring to a boil. Reduce the heat to medium-low, and allow the soup to simmer for 1½ hours.

4. Just before the soup is ready, preheat oven to 450°F. Brush a few pieces of sliced French bread with olive oil. Place on a tray, and bake for 2 minutes. Remove from the oven, top with Gruyère cheese, and bake for another minute, or until the cheese melts. Pour the soup in a bowl and top with the cheesy bread.

LE MONARQUE

- **Difficulty:** Easy
- **Prep time:** 30 minutes
- **Cook time:** 30 minutes
- **Yield:** 4 servings
- **Dietary notes:** Dairy

Oozing with cheese, this sandwich—based on an EDZ recipe known as a croque monsieur—is stacked far too tall for a regular patron to tackle in one bite. I've named my version, which piles on the cheese, meat, and bread, after the Le Monarque bow, as they're both beautiful and dangerously delicious.

Bechamel Sauce:
3 tablespoons unsalted butter
3 tablespoons flour
1 cup milk
¼ teaspoon ground nutmeg
1 teaspoon salt
1 teaspoon pepper
2 tablespoons Dijon mustard

Sandwich:
8 slices sourdough bread
½ pound sliced ham
½ cup shredded Gruyère cheese

For the bechamel sauce:

1. Preheat oven to 425°F. Place a saucepan over medium heat, and melt the butter. Add the flour, and whisk together to make a roux. Heat until the flour has cooked—it will begin to smell a bit like bread. Slowly add the milk into the saucepan while constantly whisking. Cook until the sauce has thickened. Remove from the heat. Add nutmeg, salt, pepper, and Dijon mustard, mix, and set aside.

For the sandwich:

2. Prepare a baking sheet with aluminum foil. Take each of the slices of bread, and spread one side generously with the bechamel sauce. Place 4 of the pieces, bechamel side up, on the baking sheet. Top each piece of bread with the sliced ham. Top with half of the Gruyère cheese. Top with the remaining bread slices, bechamel side up. Top with the remaining Gruyère cheese.

3. Bake the sandwiches for 10 to 15 minutes, or until the tops have slightly browned.

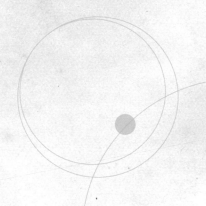

CRIMSON DAYS

If you live in the Tower, the Crimson Days are hard to miss. The entire city center is covered in beautiful petals, gorgeous red and white banners, and the distinct feeling of love is in the air. Although I'm still responsible for the different community events that take place in the Last City, Crimson Days is Shaxx's pet project. He does most of the planning of events and organizing of volunteers. My main task is to prevent him from going overboard and washing us all off the Tower in a flood of flower petals. (I'm not sure where he finds them all every year!)

The tale of how the Crimson Days celebration began goes like this: There were two Guardians, diametrically opposed, who found themselves stuck fighting for their lives. They were besieged by a previously unknown foe, the Cabal, and managed to sort out their differences in order to keep each other alive. After defeating countless enemies, they finally escaped, hand in hand, and discovered a bond they had not previously known. In spite of the dangers of combat, Shaxx hopes others will form similar bonds and carry on that same joy.

I hope everyone reading this has love in their life. Life's too short, even for Guardians, to go without finding someone special. The crimson bond that Shaxx goes on and on about doesn't need to be a romantic relationship, either. We all deserve people who care about us. So here are some beautiful recipes to share with the important people in your life. If you're feeling adventurous, make the whole list of recipes in this section for a wonderful meal.

- Difficulty: Easy
- Prep time: 15 minutes
- Yield: 6 servings
- Dietary notes: Vegetarian

SPINACH SALAD

This spinach salad is the perfect way to start a Crimson Days dinner. It's light and delicious, and the scattered strawberries are like the petals adorning the City. Be careful not to eat too much or you won't have room for the rest of the meal!

10 ounces fresh spinach

3 ounces arugula

8 ounces strawberries, hulled and quartered

1 avocado, cut into large chunks

3 ounces goat cheese, crumbled

3 ounces pecans, coarsely chopped

Shallot Vinaigrette (page 21)

1. Combine spinach and arugula in a large bowl. Transfer an equal portion to six salad bowls. Top each with strawberries, avocado, goat cheese, and pecans. Serve with Shallot Vinaigrette.

RACK OF LAMB

⬚ Difficulty: Medium

◷ Prep time: 1 hour

◉ Cook time: 30 minutes

⚠ Yield: 4 servings

▦ Dietary notes:
Dairy-Free

My favorite part of a Crimson Days dinner is the centerpiece that I always prepare, a tremendous rack of lamb. Sometimes lamb is hard to come by, so I place an order with the postmaster well ahead to make sure it'll be delivered in time. I do hope sharing this recipe doesn't make lamb even harder to find.

1 head garlic

1 fresh rosemary sprig, leaves removed from stem

1½ tablespoons Orange and Lime Rosemary Salt (page 19)

4½ teaspoons olive oil

1 teaspoon pepper

2 pounds rack of lamb

1. Combine the garlic, rosemary, Orange and Lime Rosemary Salt, olive oil, and pepper in a bowl. Rub the mixture on the lamb. Prepare a baking sheet with aluminum foil, and top with a wire rack. Place the lamb on the wire rack, fat side up. Let rest at room temperature for 45 minutes.

2. Preheat oven to 450°F. Place in the oven, and roast until the meat reaches the desired temperature:

    Medium-Rare: 125°F—25 minutes

    Medium: 135°F—30 minutes

    Medium-Well: 140°F—35 minutes

3. Turn the broiler on high and cook until the fat begins to crisp up, about 2 to 4 minutes. Remove from the oven, and cover in aluminum foil. Let rest for 10 minutes. To serve, use a sharp knife and cut portions between the bones.

HERB POTATO STACKS

- Difficulty: Easy
- Prep time: 30 minutes
- Cook time: 40 to 50 minutes
- Yield: 12 servings
- Dietary notes: Vegan

I got a little fancy with this side dish, but the presentation does wonders for the dinner table. I like to think it represents the Tower, standing over the Last City it protects. The layers on layers house all the work involved in keeping hope alive. That may sound a little silly, but presentation is important!

2 tablespoons olive oil

2 fresh rosemary sprigs, leaves removed from stem and chopped

2 fresh thyme sprigs, chopped

2 teaspoons salt

2 teaspoons pepper

2 pounds Yukon gold potatoes, skin left on and cut into ⅛-inch slices

Orange and Lime Rosemary Salt (page 19)

1 tablespoon chopped chives

1. Preheat oven to 375°F. Combine olive oil, rosemary, thyme, salt, and pepper in a large bowl. Toss the potato slices to coat. Prepare a muffin tin with nonstick spray. Stack the potato slices in each of the muffin cups, filling just to the top. Sprinkle each stack with Orange and Lime Rosemary Salt.

2. Place in the oven, and bake for 40 to 50 minutes, or until the tops are slightly golden. Turn the broiler on high, and cook for 1 to 2 minutes to give the tops a little extra crispiness. Remove from the oven, and let rest for 3 minutes. Remove the stacks from the muffin tin, and top with chives.

DARK CHOCOLATE MOTES

Difficulty: Medium
Prep time: 40 minutes
Cook time: 20 minutes
Yield: 32 servings
Dietary notes: Dairy; Tree Nuts; Vegetarian

Despite all the rumors that swirl around the Drifter—whom I do not trust!—I recognize that he's a fairly interesting and unusual character. I dedicate this delectable dessert to the many-faceted person he is.

½ cup hazelnuts
8 ounces 100 percent dark chocolate
4 ounces bittersweet chocolate
1 teaspoon ground cardamom
Flake sea salt (optional)

1. Preheat oven to 350°F. Place hazelnuts on a baking sheet, and bake for 10 minutes, or until lightly roasted. Toss occasionally.

2. Fill the bottom of double boiler pot with water, and bring to a simmer over medium-high heat. Place the chocolate in the top pot, and place over the simmering water. Mix until fully melted. Add the cardamom, and mix well.

3. To shape the motes, you will need a mini-pyramid silicone mold (each piece should be about 1 inch in size). Fill each of the molds ⅓ of the way up with chocolate. Transfer 1 hazelnut into each mold. Cover each section with chocolate. Clean up any extra chocolate, and make sure the bottom is flat. If desired, sprinkle a few sea salt flakes on the bottom of each pyramid. Place in the refrigerator for at least 2 hours. Remove from the mold, and store in an airtight container in the refrigerator for up to 2 weeks.

WHITE CHOCOLATE TRAVELERS

Difficulty: Medium
Prep time: 4 hours
Cook time: 10 minutes
Yield: 20 to 24 servings
Dietary notes:
Dairy; Vegetarian

These round white chocolate desserts are a bit time-consuming to make, but their flavor is surprisingly bright and unique. And their round shape reminds me quite a bit of the Traveler!

16 ounces white chocolate
¼ cup coconut cream
2 tablespoons unsalted butter
1 teaspoon vanilla extract
2 tablespoons orange zest
1 teaspoon salt
8 ounces vanilla candy coating

1. Combine white chocolate and coconut cream in a small saucepan over low heat. Mix together until the white chocolate has completely melted. Transfer to a bowl. Add butter, and mix until smooth. Mix in vanilla extract, orange zest, and salt. Let cool. Cover and place in the refrigerator for at least 3 hours.

2. Remove from the refrigerator and scoop out 1 tablespoon of the chocolate. Form into small 1-inch-round balls by rolling in between your hands. Place on a piece of parchment paper. Cover and place back in the refrigerator for 30 minutes.

3. Melt the vanilla candy coating according to the instructions on the packaging. Allow to cool slightly to not melt the filling. Take a filling ball and pierce with a skewer. Dip in the melted candy coating and cover completely. Allow any excess to drip off. Carefully place on parchment paper and remove the skewer. Repeat with the remaining portions. Place in the refrigerator, and allow the candy coating to harden, about 30 minutes. Transfer to an airtight container. These can be stored in the refrigerator for up to 1 week.

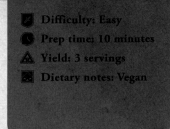
THE VOW

For Crimson Days, Shaxx made a bunch of these beautifully handcrafted combat bows that he nicknamed The Vow. He wanted to hand them out to the Guardians who proved their love on the battlefield. I had no plans on entering the Crucible and trying to earn one for myself, so I named this drink after the trophy instead.

1 tablespoon simple syrup
Juice of 1 lemon
2 tablespoons grenadine
1 tablespoon gin
Ice
15 raspberries
Champagne

1. Combine simple syrup, lemon juice, grenadine, gin, and ice in a cocktail shaker. Cover and shake for 10 seconds. Prepare 3 champagne glasses with 5 raspberries each. Strain and pour the mixture from the cocktail shaker evenly between the 3 glasses. Top with champagne.

ANA BRAY

I met with Anastasia Bray briefly on her latest visit to the Last City. She stopped by for some Crimson Days ideas to bring back with her to Mars, where she has been doing some personal research with her partner, Camrin. I gave her some of the White Chocolate Travelers that I had made recently in hopes of brightening up her holiday and the bond she shares with Camrin. She mentioned to me that she had found something in her relationship that she had never had before.

Ana has spent so much time on her own, chasing her own mysteries. Becoming a Guardian meant she lost one identity and gained another. When she chose to disappear after the Battle of Twilight Gap, she found herself caught between two selves—a member of House Bray and a Guardian—and desperate to find answers about Clovis Bray and Rasputin. It was then that she met Camrin.

I don't know what secrets lie in Ana's past, but I know that her present is with Camrin. She absolutely lights up when she speaks of her partner. I can only hope that, one day, they will both find the answers they are looking for. Maybe then they will be able to return to the City and enjoy a leisurely meal together, with a delectible Spinach Salad, a hearty Rack of Lamb, and a side of Herb Potato Stacks. Of course, they could always indulge in a few White Chocolate Travelers while enjoying a glass of The Vow as they look forward to the next chapter in their lives.

THE REVELRY

When I first created the Revelry, I wanted to bring in a more lighthearted holiday that celebrates the joys of being alive. I was a bit nervous about starting a new tradition, but everyone seemed to have a great time. Guardians had the opportunity to practice their skills in the Verdant Forest, and the fizzy Reveler's Tonic that I created was very popular. Guardians kept coming back for more, only to go dashing off to the festivities again.

I first had to conceive and pitch the idea of a new event, and I had concerns about people's availability given all the danger present in our little corner of the universe. But I figured that giving people the opportunity to relax and take some time for themselves is just as important as war preparations. Zavala, of course, thought the very idea was preposterous. Thankfully, Tess came to the rescue and helped get the event off the ground. She even funded some of the activities and created the beautiful helmet ornaments that all the Guardians were showing off.

For the festivities, I wanted to put together a set of snacks and drinks that everyone would enjoy, whether they were a Guardian taking a break between ventures into the Verdant Forest or a citizen of the Last City enjoying the festivities. Tess and I love having afternoon tea, so I thought small sandwiches and bite-size treats would be perfect. Don't just make some of these dishes on a whim though; set some time aside to sit down and really enjoy them. Devrim taught me that tea should always be enjoyed at leisure, and I'd be remiss to disregard that man's dining etiquette.

FINGER SANDWICHES

Difficulty: Easy

Prep time: 30 minutes

Yield: 12 to 18 sandwiches

Dietary notes: Dairy

I've done my best to prepare the Guardians who enjoy the challenge of the Verdant Forest. I am so proud of the dedication of each and every Guardian, but I worry that some push themselves too hard. I've started handing these out to those who appear in need of some encouragement and fortitude as they continue their trek through the Forest.

Lemon Butter:

¼ cup unsalted butter, softened

Zest of 1 lemon

1 teaspoon fresh chives, finely diced

1 teaspoon salt

Sandwiches:

8 pieces white or pumpernickel bread, sliced

½ cup cream cheese, softened

4 small cucumbers, peeled and thinly sliced

4 ounces smoked salmon

For the lemon butter:

1. Combine all the ingredients for the lemon butter and set aside.

For the sandwiches:

2. Take two slices of bread. On one slice, spread a light portion of cream cheese and top with cucumber and smoked salmon. On the other slice of bread, spread a small portion of the lemon butter. Put slices together. Cut off the crusts, cut into rectangles, and form small sandwiches. Repeat until all the sandwiches have been made.

BEET-PICKLED DEVILED EGGS

- **Difficulty: Medium**
- **Prep time: 4 hours**
- **Cook time: 45 minutes**
- **Yield: 16 deviled eggs**
- **Dietary notes: Dairy-Free; Eggs**

These deviled eggs are bright and vibrant, both in color and flavor, and they complement the Vernal Growth armor beautifully. Share these with your friends as you celebrate the Revelry.

Marinated Eggs:
8 eggs
½ cup apple cider vinegar
¼ cup rice wine vinegar
2 cups water
1 tablespoon sugar
2 teaspoons salt
1 cooked beet, peeled and quartered

Filling:
1 ripe avocado, peeled and pitted
1 tablespoon fresh chives, chopped
1 tablespoon lime juice
1 teaspoon lime zest
Salt and pepper

Topping:
1 piece thick prosciutto

For the marinated eggs:

1. Place the eggs in a medium saucepan, and cover them completely with cold water. Cover with a lid and place over medium-high heat. Bring to a boil, and boil for 7 minutes.

2. Once the timer for the eggs goes off, immediately take the pot off the stove and place it under cold running water. Move the eggs to a bowl with ice cubes and cold water. Let sit for 3 minutes. Carefully remove the shells of the eggs and set aside.

3. Combine the vinegars, water, sugar, salt, and beet in a medium saucepan over medium-high heat. Bring to a boil. Reduce the heat to medium-low, and simmer for 15 minutes.

4. Transfer the liquid into a large sealable glass container, and allow to cool completely. Add the eggs, and make sure they are completely submerged. Refrigerate the container for a minimum of 3 hours to a maximum of 8 hours.

For the filling:

5. Remove the eggs from the mixture and pat dry. Cut the eggs in half. Place the egg yolks in a bowl and smash slightly. Add the avocado to the egg yolks. Stir in the chives, lime juice, and lime zest. Fill the halved eggs with the filling. Season with salt and pepper to taste.

For the topping:

6. Place a pan over high heat. Add nonstick spray, and cook the prosciutto until both sides have crisped up. Cut the prosciutto into 16 pieces, and garnish each of the deviled eggs with 1 piece.

CHOCOLATE PALMIERS

◈ **Difficulty: Easy**
◔ **Prep time: 30 minutes**
◊ **Cook time: 20 minutes**
△ **Yield: 24 cookies**
◈ **Dietary notes: Dairy; Vegetarian**

I had a hard time understanding what the Verdant Forest was until I heard it compared to a palmier: time, folded in on itself over and over again, covered in chocolate. On second thought, perhaps I still don't quite understand it.

¼ cup sugar
1½ teaspoons Vanilla Cinnamon Salt
  (page 19)
2 sheets puff pastry, thawed
8 ounces bittersweet chocolate

1. Preheat oven to 400°F. Combine the sugar and Vanilla Cinnamon Salt in a small bowl. Lay one of the puff pastry sheets out on the counter. Sprinkle with the sugar and salt mixture.

2. Roll both ends of the pastry to the center. Wrap tightly in plastic wrap. Repeat those steps with the second sheet of puff pastry. Place in the freezer, and let them rest for 15 minutes.

3. Carefully cut the rolled puff pastry into ¾-inch-thick pieces. Lay the cut pieces on a baking sheet with the cut sides facing up. Make sure to give the pieces enough room to puff while they bake. Bake for 15 minutes or until golden brown. Set aside to cool.

4. Place the chocolate in a bowl and heat in the microwave, stirring every 30 seconds, until completely melted and smooth. Once cooled, partly dip the top of each palmier in the chocolate, and place on a wire rack to set.

GENTLEMAN'S SHORTBREAD

Difficulty: Medium
Prep time: 45 minutes
Cook time: 20 minutes
Yield: 10 scones
Dietary notes: Dairy; Vegetarian

I'll never forget the kindness Devrim showed me after the Red War, checking in at the Farm from time to time and sitting down with me for a cup of tea. These days, I occasionally send him my favorite shortbread as a thank-you for his thoughtfulness, knowing it will pair wonderfully with his tea.

3 cups all-purpose flour

1 teaspoon ground cardamom

1 teaspoon salt

¼ cup sugar

1½ tablespoon baking powder

½ cup European-style butter,
   cubed and cold

½ teaspoon vanilla extract

1 cup milk

1 egg

2 teaspoons water

Clotted cream, for serving

Jam, for serving

1. Preheat oven to 425°F. Combine the flour, cardamom, salt, sugar, and baking powder in a large bowl. Add the cubed butter, and combine with your hands until mixture resembles coarse cornmeal.

2. Add the vanilla extract and milk, and stir until the dough becomes workable. Transfer to a floured countertop, and knead until the dough just comes together. Make sure to not overwork the dough. Gently pat the dough into a 1-inch-tall disc. Cut into ten 3-inch-round scones.

3. Place on a baking sheet with parchment paper, and refrigerate for 15 minutes. Whisk together the egg and water. Brush each of the scones with the mixture. Bake for 13 to 18 minutes or until golden brown. Transfer to a wire rack and allow to cool. Serve with clotted cream and your favorite jam.

LONDON FOG

- ⚔ Difficulty: Easy
- ⏱ Prep time: 15 minutes
- 🔥 Cook time: 10 minutes
- ⚠ Yield: 2 cups
- ⬛ Dietary notes: Dairy-Free

It's no secret that Devrim loves tea. I've shared this delightful recipe with him because it provides an interesting twist on his usual cuppa. The sweetness of the honey and the nuttiness of the almond milk make this drink soothing and delicious.

2 Earl Grey tea bags
2 to 3 tablespoons honey
2 cups almond milk
1 tablespoon vanilla extract

1. Boil 1½ cups of water. Place the tea bags and honey in a large cup—use 3 tablespoons of honey if you prefer it to be sweet—and pour in the boiling water. Steep the tea for 5 to 7 minutes.

2. While tea steeps, heat the almond milk in a medium saucepan over medium heat. Bring to a simmer for 5 minutes. Remove from the heat, and whisk in the vanilla extract. Transfer to a blender. Blend on medium-high until the milk becomes frothy, about 5 minutes.

3. Split the steeped tea into 2 cups. Fill each glass with frothed milk.

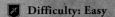
Difficulty: Easy
Prep time: 5 minutes
Yield: 1 cup
Dietary notes: Vegan

REVELER'S TONIC

I'm not quite ready to give out the recipe for my original Reveler's Tonic that so many Guardians loved, so I threw together this new version of my famous fizzy drink to get everyone in the holiday spirit. I heard, though, that things got slightly out of hand. The Guardians who had a bit too much wound up challenging each other to do increasingly wild acrobatics off flagpoles and drapery—and even leaping off the Tower. They made quite a ruckus! Of course, I do not begrudge any Guardian the freedom to let loose and enjoy life. Finding joy is so important.

2 tablespoons apple juice
2 teaspoons nonalcoholic curaçao
2 teaspoons lime juice
Ice
Sparkling grape juice

1. Combine the apple juice, curaçao, and lime juice in a cocktail shaker filled with ice. Cover and shake vigorously for 10 seconds. Strain, pour into a champagne flute, and top with sparkling grape juice.

FESTIVAL OF THE LOST

I love planning and celebrating all the Tower holidays, but one of the most meaningful events is the Festival of the Lost. With candy, masks, and dancing, the festivities might seem whimsical and silly, but please remember that they are also much more than that. I brought this holiday to the Tower because we've all experienced loss—some more recently than others—and we should spend some time reflecting and commemorating those who are gone from our lives. If you are a Guardian reading this, you may not remember your past, but someone lost you long ago. Not celebrating what we still have does a disservice to the spirits of the past.

I couldn't have a section of this book that was dedicated to just candy, so I got some inspiration from my research into the Golden Age. Back then, a holiday similar to the Festival of the Lost called the Day of the Dead was celebrated. Families would get together to pray and remember those who had passed, hoping they were happy in the afterlife. What would they think of our Guardians and the way they defy death at every turn? Would the Light of the Traveler be seen as a blessing or a curse?

In this section are some examples of food and drink enjoyed in times long past. I hope you'll spend some time during this year's Festival of the Lost reflecting on how much we as a people have dealt with—not just you and me, but also everyone else you come across. Treat each other kindly, and remember to have some candy ready for those going door-to-door. Oh, and please don't hand out celery like some people have done in the past!

TORTILLA CHICKEN SOUP

⚔ **Difficulty: Easy**
🕐 **Prep time: 1 hour**
🔥 **Cook time: 30 minutes**
⚠ **Yield: 8 servings**
▨ **Dietary notes: Dairy**

Ramos shared this recipe with me when we reunited at the Tower after the Red War, noting that he wanted to pass on his family recipe from one uhoela to another. That boy is so sweet. I should thank him again: This dish will be perfect for warming up these old bones of mine when the winds start tearing across the open areas of the Tower.

Tortilla Chips:
8 corn tortillas, cut into strips
2 tablespoons peanut oil
Salt

Soup:
1 yellow onion, minced
2 celery stalks, cut into chunks
3 Roma tomatoes
4 cloves garlic
1 tomatillo
1 dried ancho chile, seeds removed and torn into pieces
2 corn tortillas
2 teaspoons cumin
1 tablespoon chili powder
¼ teaspoon cayenne pepper
2 quarts Chicken Broth (page 25)
Salt
Pepper
Chicken breast, shredded (from Chicken Broth)
15-ounce can black beans, drained and rinsed
11-ounce can southwestern corn

Toppings:
See list on the right

For the tortilla chips:

1. Preheat oven to 375°F. Toss the corn tortilla strips with the peanut oil in a large bowl. Prepare a baking sheet with nonstick spray. Transfer the tortillas to the baking pan in a single layer.

2. Sprinkle generously with salt. Place in the oven, and bake for 15 minutes. Rotate the pan halfway through the cooking time. Occasionally turn the strips with a spatula. Once the strips are crispy, remove and let cool. Store in an airtight container for up to 3 days.

For the soup:

3. Preheat oven broiler. Place onion, celery, tomatoes, garlic, and tomatillo on a baking sheet. Put the baking sheet under the broiler, and cook until the tomatillos have charred slightly, about 10 minutes. Transfer the charred vegetables to a blender. Add the dried ancho chile and tortillas. Blend until smooth.

4. Transfer into a large pot. Place over medium-high heat, and warm for 5 minutes. Add all the spices and broth. Season with salt and pepper to taste. Add the shredded chicken breast, black beans, and southwestern corn. Bring to a simmer, and reduce the heat to medium-low. Allow to simmer for 20 minutes.

For assembly:

5. To serve, scoop a portion of the soup and then add all of the toppings:
  - Avocados, sliced
  - Queso fresco, crumbled
  - Roasted poblano peppers, seeds removed and sliced
  - Radishes, thinly sliced
  - Scallions, chopped
  - Cilantro, chopped
  - Limes, quartered
  - Tortilla Chips

CHILES EN NOGADA

🛡 Difficulty:
Very Difficult

🕐 Prep time: 2½ hours

🔥 Cook time: 1 hour

⚠ Yield: 8 servings

🏔 Dietary notes:
Tree Nuts

I'm enamored by the tradition I found in the archives of going door-to-door and collecting candy from strangers celebrating another holiday called Hallowe'en. Unfortunately, not everyone in the Tower is as big of a fan. The first year I sent Guardians out to collect candy from everyone, a few of them came back disappointed that a member of the Vanguard only gave them boxes of raisins. I ended up with so many raisins that I came up with this delicious recipe to use them all.

Walnut Sauce:
1½ cups walnuts
2 ounces goat cheese
2 tablespoons sugar
¼ cup crema mexicana
½ cup coconut milk
½ teaspoon ground cinnamon
½ teaspoon pepper
½ teaspoon salt

Filling:
2 tablespoons canola oil
½ yellow onion, diced
2 cloves garlic, chopped
1 pound ground beef
1 pound ground pork
1 teaspoon ground cinnamon
1 tablespoon sugar
2 teaspoons thyme
1 tablespoon oregano
Salt and pepper
15-ounce can diced tomatoes
1 apple, peeled and chopped
1 pear, peeled and chopped
1 peach, peeled and chopped
¼ cup golden raisins
3 tablespoons almonds, chopped

Serving:
12 poblano peppers, roasted and
   skin removed
½ cup pomegranate seeds

For the walnut sauce:

1. Place the walnuts in a food processor, and pulse until crumbled. Add the remaining ingredients for the sauce, and pulse until smooth, about 1 minute. Transfer to an airtight container. The sauce can be stored in the refrigerator for 1 week. Before serving, take out the sauce and let sit at room temperature for 30 minutes.

For the filling:

2. Place a large pan with canola oil over medium-high heat. Add onions, and cook until softened, about 5 minutes. Add garlic, and cook for about 1 minute. Add the ground beef and pork, and cook until no longer pink, about 8 minutes. Add all of the spices, including salt and pepper to taste, and mix well. Add the diced tomatoes, apple, pear, peach, golden raisins, and almonds. Mix together. Cover and allow to simmer for 20 minutes. Set aside until the poblanos are ready to stuff.

For assembly:

3. Preheat oven to 350°F. Carefully split the poblanos lengthwise on one side and remove the seeds. Make sure to leave the stems on and to not split the poblanos completely open.

4. If you want to hide the split, load the poblanos with the filling until almost filled. Place on a deep baking dish with the split side down. If you want your poblanos to be overfilled, load the poblanos with the filling until just full. Place on a deep baking dish split side up. Add a few more scoops of filling on top. Place in the oven, and bake for 10 minutes or until warmed up.

5. To serve, place a poblano on a plate. Pour the walnut sauce widthwise across the center of the poblano. Make sure to let some of the sauce drizzle on the plate. Top with pomegranate seeds.

ELOTES

⚔ Difficulty: Easy
🕐 Prep time: 45 minutes
🔥 Cook time: 15 minutes
⚠ Yield: 5 servings
🖼 Dietary notes:
Dairy; Vegetarian

I adore the idea of street food, and many cultures prior to the Collapse had their own take on this concept. In what was once known as Latin America, they served a dish called Elote. Also known as roasted corn, it was traditionally served either on a stick or shucked into a cup for easy eating while enjoying a walk around town. What better time to take your snacks on the go than during the Festival of the Lost? Just be sure to take your masks off first.

⅔ cup mayonnaise

2 tablespoons sour cream

1 teaspoon salt

½ teaspoon chili powder

Pinch of cayenne pepper

½ teaspoon paprika, plus additional
    for garnish

Juice of 1 lime

2 tablespoons fresh cilantro,
    finely chopped

2 scallions, white and light green parts
    only, finely chopped

4 ounces queso asadero

1 tablespoon unsalted butter

4 cups corn

1 small jalapeño, seeds removed and
    finely chopped

2 ounces queso cotija

Lime slices, for garnish

1. Combine mayo, sour cream, salt, chili powder, cayenne pepper, paprika, lime juice, cilantro, scallions, and queso asadero in a medium bowl.

2. Place a skillet with butter over medium-high heat. Add the corn and jalapeño. Cook and stir for 10 to 15 minutes, or until the corn has started to brown. Transfer to the bowl, and mix well. Split the corn mixture into serving containers, and top each with queso cotija, a lime slice, and paprika.

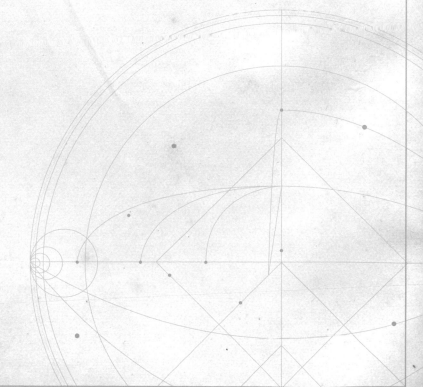

RADIOLARIAN PUDDING

⬒ **Difficulty:** Medium

🕐 **Prep time:** 30 minutes

🔥 **Cook time:** 45 minutes

⚠ **Yield:** 4 servings

▨ **Dietary notes:** Vegan

There's a strange man who goes by Asher Mir out on Io with whom Ikora communicates from time to time. We had a bit of an incident years ago, but I'll spare you the details. I made him this dessert as a thank-you because the pudding's color and texture are reminiscent of a particular substance that I'll leave unnamed.

½ cup white rice

2 cups almond milk

1 cinnamon stick

1 star anise

2 cardamom pods

½ vanilla bean, split in half, seeds removed and set aside

1 teaspoon salt

3 tablespoons sugar

1 strip of orange peel

2 strips of lime peel

1 tablespoon coconut oil

1 tablespoon maple syrup

1. Combine the rice, almond milk, cinnamon stick, star anise, cardamom pods, vanilla bean pod and seeds, salt, sugar, orange peel, and lime peels in a 2-quart saucepan over medium-high heat. Bring to a boil. Reduce the heat to medium-low, and cover.

2. Simmer for 30 minutes, or until the rice is cooked and most of the liquid evaporates. Make sure to stir frequently while cooking so the rice doesn't stick to the bottom of the pan.

3. Remove from the heat. Remove the cinnamon stick, star anise, cardamom pods, vanilla bean pod, orange peel, and lime peels. Stir in coconut oil and maple syrup. Serve hot, or refrigerate and serve cold.

SKYBURNER'S OATH

Difficulty: Easy
Prep time: 10 minutes
Cook time: 20 minutes
Yield: 2 servings
Dietary notes: Dairy

At the first Festival of the Lost that I celebrated after the Red War, I served some delicious spiced hot chocolate. A few Guardians stopped by for a mug and shared with me the stories of those they lost to the Cabal. The Awoken pulled a scout rifle out of his holster and said the weapon, Skyburner's Oath, was the reason he lived to tell the tale of his fallen comrades. But that day, the hot chocolate was exactly what he needed, and he bequeathed it with the same name.

2½ cups milk
¾ cup heavy cream
⅓ cup sugar
2 tablespoons cocoa powder
1 teaspoon ground cinnamon
½ teaspoon cayenne pepper
½ teaspoon chili powder
½ teaspoon salt
2 ounces dark chocolate, chopped
2 teaspoons vanilla extract
Marshmallows (page 27)

1. Combine milk, heavy cream, sugar, cocoa powder, cinnamon, cayenne pepper, chili powder, and salt in a saucepan over medium heat. Once lightly boiling, add the chopped chocolate and vanilla extract. Whisk until the chocolate melts. Serve with Marshmallows. Optionally, use a kitchen torch to lightly char the Marshmallows.

HORROR STORY

⚔ Difficulty: Easy

🕐 Prep time: 12 hours

⚠ Yield: 8 servings

▦ Dietary notes: Vegan

I heard Amanda gave out an auto-rifle called the Horror Story when she was running the Festival of the Lost all by herself, and I really regret not being there to help. I have this recipe for a delectable horchata that would have gone with it perfectly. Oh, and I would have called it Horrorchata Story, too. A good pun is such a terrible thing to waste, so I'll leave it here in this cookbook.

1⅓ cups white rice

2 cinnamon sticks

3 cups water

⅓ cup sugar

4 cups almond milk

2 tablespoons vanilla extract

1 cup coconut cream

1 vanilla bean, split in half, seeds removed and set aside

1. Combine the rice, cinnamon sticks, and water in a bowl. Cover and place in the refrigerator overnight.

2. Transfer the contents of the bowl into a blender. Add sugar, and blend until completely smooth, which can take more than 2 minutes. Transfer the liquid into a pitcher through a mesh strainer. Add a cheesecloth to the strainer if you want the drink to be less gritty. You might have to pass the liquid a few times through the strainer to remove the grittiness.

3. Once the consistency is to your liking, add almond milk, vanilla extract, coconut cream, and vanilla seeds, and mix well. This drink can be stored in the refrigerator up to 1 week.

THE DRIFTER

The Drifter is certainly one of the more . . . *interesting* characters I've run across in my travels. I'm not a fan of him, but sometimes I think he prefers it that way. I have had only a couple of short conversations with him, and he has briefly mentioned his bar before changing the subject. I did finally manage to get his recipe for Banh Mi Burgers out of him, though. It's an excellent addition to my repertoire, especially because he's out of the restaurant business now.

Despite those "friendly" moments, I can't shake the feeling that I can't or shouldn't trust him. I was walking through a part of the Tower I don't normally go when I overheard the Drifter mention something about "jerky" to a Guardian. It's no business of mine, but if he thinks he has a better jerky recipe than me, I'd like to see him try. But I have a feeling that wasn't what he was referencing.

On the other hand, I certainly can't claim to know everything about the Drifter. You'll never believe it—I barely believe it myself—but I think I saw him getting into the Crimson Days spirit. He was sporting a maintenance vest and had a trash bag in hand (who knows where he got either) and was helping clean up after a successful celebration. It was miraculous to see even someone as distant as him find joy in the holiday.

If I were to ever put together a menu to sit down and share with the Drifter, I would make it as eclectic as his own travels: Duck Poutine, Banh Mi Burgers, Elotes, Dark Chocolate Motes, and a glass of Thorn. After all, who really knows all that this man has seen and done in his life?

THE DAWNING

The Dawning is one of my favorite times of the year. I came up with the idea years ago: a festive holiday for celebrating each other by combining a few old traditions from before the Collapse. There's gift giving, wishing each other good health and good luck, and even some beautiful lights in the sky. Ikora usually helps me with the decorations, assuming she can spare the time. As the winter season approaches, the weather can be so cruel on these old bones. The warm greetings and holiday cheer more than make up for it.

Because I have so much to do during the Dawning, I've had to delegate some of my responsibilities. Of all the people willing to give me a hand, one particular Guardian volunteering to spare some time was most unexpected. I lent them one of my family's prized possessions, a portable oven I thought I had lost during the Red War, and gave them a list of gifts to bake and deliver all around the solar system. Much to my surprise, they did a fantastic job. They even somehow improved the oven I lent them, imbuing it with what feels like the Traveler's Light. I didn't ask how they did it, but I'm happy that everyone got their Dawning treats.

This Dawning, take some time to bring some extra cheer to your friends and neighbors. Oftentimes I can't settle into the holiday spirit until I've shared some love with the people closest to me. And one of the best ways to do so is to cook for them, so here are recipes for some of my most delicious Dawning treats. I don't have enough special holiday ovens to lend out, but I think these recipes should be manageable with your oven at home. And if you happen to run into that Guardian this Dawning, be sure to give them a thanks from me for all their help.

GJALLARDOODLES

Difficulty: Easy
Prep time: 1 hour
Cook time: 20 minutes
Yield: 20 cookies
Dietary notes: Dairy; Tree Nuts; Vegetarian

You most likely know how stern and cold Zavala presents himself. It wasn't until I celebrated my first Dawning at the Tower that I learned how kind hearted he can be. I was making a batch of these cookies when he stopped by to tell me a joke. It was quite an awkward retelling, and frankly I can't remember the punch line, but he seemed so much more . . . relaxed after that. Since then, I make sure to whip up a batch of these for him every year.

¾ cup plus ⅓ cup whole cashews, divided
2½ cups all-purpose flour
½ teaspoon salt
1½ teaspoons baking powder
1 cup unsalted butter, room temperature
¾ cup sugar
2 teaspoons vanilla extract
1 egg white

1. Place ¾ cup of the whole cashews on a baking sheet. Bake for 10 to 15 minutes, or until the nuts have browned. Transfer to a food processor, and grind until fine.

2. Combine the ground cashews, flour, salt, and baking powder in a small bowl. Cream the butter in a large bowl, and mix until smooth. Add the sugar, and mix until well incorporated. Add the vanilla extract and egg white.

3. Add the flour mixture in two batches, until just combined. Place a sheet of plastic wrap on a counter, and transfer the dough on top. Lightly press the dough into a square shape, and then wrap. Use a rolling pin to flatten the dough. Place in the freezer for 10 minutes.

4. Prepare a baking sheet with parchment paper. Remove the dough from the freezer and plastic wrap onto a lightly floured counter. Lightly place the plastic wrap on top of the dough, and roll out the dough until it is ½ inch thick. Use a 2-inch-round cookie cutter and cut out cookies. Transfer the cut cookies to the baking sheet. Split the remaining ⅓ cup whole cashews in half. Press a cashew half into the center of the cookies. Place the baking sheet into the freezer for 10 minutes.

5. Preheat oven to 350°F. Place in the oven and bake for 15 to 18 minutes, or until golden brown.

CHOCOLATE SHIP COOKIES

- Difficulty: Medium
- Prep time: 3 hours
- Cook time: 15 to 17 minutes
- Yield: 28 cookies
- Dietary notes: Dairy; Eggs; Vegetarian; Tree Nuts (Optional)

My research shows that chocolate chip cookies were one of the most popular treats of the Golden Age. There were many competing recipes in the logs, but my rendition is without a doubt the best. I know Amanda Holliday is very much a fan!

1 cup unsalted butter
1¼ cups dark brown sugar
½ cup white sugar
2 eggs
1 tablespoon vanilla extract
1 cup bread flour
¾ cup all-purpose flour
1½ teaspoons baking soda
2 teaspoons salt
2 cups whole-rolled oats
8 ounces dark chocolate, chopped
½ cup walnuts (optional)

1. Melt the butter in a saucepan over medium heat. Cook while occasionally swirling the butter until it becomes golden brown, about 10 minutes. Pour the butter into a cup, and let it cool.

2. In a large bowl, place the butter, dark brown sugar, and white sugar, and mix. Add the eggs and vanilla extract. Scrape the sides and bottom of the bowl as needed. In a small bowl, combine the bread flour, all-purpose flour, baking soda, salt, and oats. Slowly mix into the wet ingredients until well combined. Fold in the chocolate chips and walnuts.

3. Place parchment paper on a baking sheet. Split the dough into 50-gram-size dough balls, and place on the parchment paper. Cover with plastic wrap and let rest in the refrigerator for at least 1 hour, up to a max of 2 days. If you are not baking these yet, place in a ziplock bag, and put in the freezer for up to 2 months.

4. Preheat oven to 350°F. Cover a baking sheet with parchment paper and nonstick spray. Place the cookies on the prepared baking sheet with 2 inches of space between each. Bake for 15 to 17 minutes (if frozen, add 1 to 2 minutes), rotating the pan once during baking. Allow to cool completely.

ALKANE DRAGÉE COOKIES

⚔ **Difficulty: Easy**

🕐 **Prep time: 45 minutes**

🔥 **Cook time: 20 to 25 minutes**

⚠ **Yield: 36 cookies**

▨ **Dietary notes: Dairy; Tree Nuts; Vegetarian**

I sent a version of these cookies to Sloane and her crew during the last Dawning. It sounds like they were the perfect way to close out a feast among the haphazard platforms of Siren's Watch and bring a little brightness to the holiday. Since then, I've augmented this recipe with a bit of almond extract to add a little more flavor to the cookies.

1¾ cups all-purpose flour

1 cup almond flour

1 teaspoon baking powder

1 teaspoon Vanilla Cinnamon Salt (page 19)

1 cup unsalted butter, softened

1¼ cups confectioners' sugar, plus more for dusting

1 egg

1 teaspoon almond extract

1 tablespoon vanilla extract

1 cup sliced almonds

1. Preheat oven to 350°F. Combine the all-purpose flour, almond flour, baking powder, and Vanilla Cinnamon Salt in a small bowl, and set aside. In a large bowl, cream the butter, and mix until smooth. Add the confectioners' sugar in batches, and mix until fluffy.

2. Mix in the egg, almond extract, and vanilla extract. Add the flour mixture in three batches, until just combined. Add the sliced almonds, and mix until fully incorporated.

3. Line a baking sheet with parchment paper. Take a tablespoon of the cookie dough (25 grams) and roll it into a ball. Place on baking sheet. Repeat until all the dough is transferred. Place in the refrigerator for 30 minutes. Gently press the balls of dough down on the parchment paper. Place in the oven and bake for 15 to 20 minutes, or until golden brown.

4. Transfer the cookies to a wire rack, and dust with confectioners' sugar while still warm.

VANILLA BLADES

- Difficulty: Medium
- Prep time: 45 minutes
- Cook time: 45 minutes
- Yield: 12 to 14 cookies
- Dietary notes: Dairy; Eggs; Vegetarian

As loud as a fusion rifle, Shaxx may seem like a brute, but he cares deeply for those whom he looks after. I made him these cookies during the Dawning as thanks for his kindness because both their crispness and blade shape remind me so much of him.

2 cups all-purpose flour

2 teaspoons baking powder

½ teaspoon salt

5 tablespoons unsalted butter, softened

¾ cup sugar

2 eggs

2 teaspoons vanilla extract

1 vanilla bean, split, seeds removed and set aside

2 tablespoons orange zest

1. Preheat oven to 350°F. Combine flour, baking powder, and salt in a small bowl, and set aside. In a large bowl, cream the butter and sugar, and mix until smooth. Add eggs one at a time. Mix in the vanilla extract, vanilla bean seeds, and orange zest. Mix in the flour until it just comes together.

2. Line a baking sheet with parchment paper and place the dough on top. Form into a log ¾ inch tall by 5½ inches wide by 9½ inches long. Bake for 25 to 30 minutes, or until the log firms up.

3. Remove from the oven, let the cookie cool for 15 minutes, and reduce the heat to 325°F. Cut the cookie, widthwise, into ½-inch-thick slices. Lay them flat on the baking sheet, and bake for 7 minutes. Flip and bake for an additional 7 minutes, then transfer to a wire rack to cool.

BURNT-EDGE TRANSIT

- Difficulty: Medium
- Prep time: 1½ hours
- Cook time: 1 hour
- Yield: 5 servings
- Dietary notes: Dairy; Vegetarian

If I ever come across something in the Golden Age archives that I don't under- I can always rely on Master Rahool to help decipher the meaning behind the engrams. To show my gratitude for his assistance, I made this treat especially for him. When I gifted them to him, I joked that he had to decrypt what was hidden under the hard sugar layer. He certainly got a chuckle out of that one.

½ cup black sesame seeds

½ cup honey

2 teaspoons almond extract

7 egg yolks

2 teaspoons Vanilla Cinnamon Salt (page 19)

2 cups heavy cream

¼ cup sugar, plus additional for serving

1. Place the black sesame seeds in a food processor, and pulse until smooth. Add honey and almond extract, and mix until it forms a smooth paste. This can be stored in an airtight container in the refrigerator for up to 2 days.

2. Preheat oven to 325°F. Combine the black sesame paste, egg yolks, and Vanilla Cinnamon Salt in a large bowl. Combine heavy cream and sugar in a saucepan over medium-high heat. Bring to a simmer for 10 minutes. Carefully and slowly pour the heated cream into the large bowl while constantly whisking. Split the batter between 5 ramekins.

3. Place the ramekins inside a deep baking dish. Fill the dish with water about halfway up the sides of the ramekins. Place in the oven, and bake for 35 to 45 minutes, or until the edges are set but the centers jiggle slightly. Remove from the oven, and take the ramekins out of the baking dish. Let them cool to room temperature. Once completely cooled, place the ramekins in the refrigerator for at least 3 hours.

4. Before serving, sprinkle the top of the crème brûlées with sugar. Use a torch to melt and caramelize the sugar until amber in color.

INFINITE FOREST CAKE

Difficulty: Hard

Prep time: 24 hours

Cook time: 2 hours

Yield: 1 cake

Dietary notes: Dairy; Eggs; Vegetarian

I heard from a Guardian returning from Nessus that a fail-safe from one of those Exodus ships of yore is still around and that it was taught to wish everyone a happy Dawning! I know full well that a ship AI can't eat cake, but anyone who is in the Dawning spirit deserves a treat. This chocolate and cherry cake is a rich delight created for that purpose. I just need to find someone who can resist eating it long enough to deliver it for me.

Cherry Filling:
¾ pound cherries, pitted and cut
  in half
2 tablespoons water
3 tablespoons honey
¼ cup sugar

Cake:
¾ cup cocoa powder
⅓ cup cherry fruit spread
¾ cup hot water
2 cups all-purpose flour
1 teaspoon baking soda
1 teaspoon baking powder
1 teaspoon salt
1 cup unsalted butter, softened
1½ cups sugar
2 eggs, room temperature
1 tablespoon vanilla extract
¾ cup sour cream

Frosting:
1½ cups unsalted butter, softened
16 ounces cream cheese, softened
½ tablespoon vanilla extract
¼ cup maraschino cherry liqueur
4 cups confectioners' sugar

Toppings:
Fresh cherries

For the cherry filling:

1. The night before, combine cherries, water, honey, and sugar in a saucepan. Bring to a boil, and reduce to a simmer for 30 minutes. Cook until the liquid has reduced by ¼. Place the mixture in a bowl, cover, and allow to rest in the refrigerator overnight.

For the cake:

2. Preheat oven to 350°F. Whisk together cocoa powder, cherry fruit spread, and hot water in a small bowl. In another bowl, combine the flour, baking soda, baking powder, and salt.

3. Cream the butter and sugar in a large bowl until smooth. Add the eggs one at a time. Mix in vanilla extract. Add the cocoa powder mixture. Mix in half of the flour mixture until it just comes together. Mix in the sour cream. Add the remainder of the flour mixture, and mix until fully combined.

4. Spray two 9-inch baking pans with nonstick spray. Split the batter between the two pans and place in the oven to bake for 25 to 30 minutes, or until done. Remove the cakes from the baking pans, and allow to cool completely.

For the frosting:

5. Place the butter and cream cheese in a large bowl, and mix together. Add the vanilla extract and maraschino cherry liqueur. Once mixed together, begin to slowly add the confectioners' sugar. Whisk until the frosting thickens.

For assembly:

6. To assemble the cake, make sure both cake layers are level. Place the bottom layer on a plate, and top with a portion of the frosting. Add the cherry filling in the center, spreading it close to the edge but not all the way. Cover the filling with additional frosting. Top with the other layer of cake and then the remaining frosting. Decorate with fresh cherries on top.

TRAVELER DONUT HOLES

- Difficulty: Easy
- Prep time: 30 minutes
- Cook time: 8 to 12 minutes per batch
- Yield: 40 to 50 donut holes
- Dietary notes: Dairy; Vegetarian; Eggs

Ikora never seems to take a break, even when the Dawning is fast approaching. I came up with a recipe for these little donut holes so that she would have a quick dessert to eat between all the things that keep her busy. They look like little Travelers to me—though they're a bit more whole than the one floating above the Tower.

Donuts:

2 cups flour

2 teaspoons ground cardamom

1 teaspoon ground cinnamon

½ teaspoon allspice

1 cup sugar

2 teaspoons baking powder

1 teaspoon baking soda

⅓ teaspoon salt

1 cup coconut milk

2 eggs

¼ cup honey

2 tablespoons unsalted butter, melted and cooled

1 tablespoon vanilla extract

Toppings:

½ cup powdered sugar

2 teaspoons ground cardamom

1. Preheat oven to 350°F. Combine flour, cardamom, cinnamon, allspice, sugar, baking powder, baking soda, and salt in a large bowl. Whisk together the coconut milk, eggs, honey, butter, and vanilla extract in a small bowl. Whisk the wet ingredients into the dry ingredients.

2. Use nonstick spray on a donut hole baking sheet. Fill each hole ¾ of the way full with the batter. Bake for 8 to 12 minutes. Remove the donut holes from the pan and allow to slightly cool. Combine powdered sugar and cardamom in a large sealable bag. Once the donut holes have slightly cooled, place in the sealable bag and shake until fully coated. Repeat with the remaining batter. The donut holes can be stored in an airtight container, but the powdered sugar will get absorbed within a day.

ABOUT BUNGIE

Since 1991, Bungie has forged a reputation as a worldwide entertainment phenomenon by building worlds that inspire friendship. Through the combination of cutting-edge technology, beautiful art, engaging storytelling, and action-packed gameplay, Bungie has brought millions of players together. In 2014, they unveiled a new world in the form of *Destiny*—a wild frontier ripe for exploration and discovery.

SPECIAL THANKS

To the Destiny community, you've become the main characters in the stories we tell. You've filled our worlds with light and your friendship. Thank you for your passion for our games and for each other. Most of all, thank you for playing.

Special thanks to the whole team at Bungie for helping to make this book possible!

INSIGHT EDITIONS

PO Box 3088
San Rafael, CA 94912
www.insighteditions.com

f Find us on Facebook: www.facebook.com/InsightEditions
🐦 Follow us on Twitter: @insighteditions

www.bungie.net

Library of Congress Cataloging-in-Publication Data available.

ISBN: 978-1-64722-177-5

Publisher: Raoul Goff
President: Kate Jerome
Associate Publisher: Vanessa Lopez
Creative Director: Chrissy Kwasnik
VP of Manufacturing: Alix Nicholaeff
Designer: Lola Villanueva
Editor: Amanda Ng
Editorial Assistant: Maya Alpert
Managing Editor: Lauren LePera
Production Editor: Jennifer Bentham
Senior Production Manager: Greg Steffen

ROOTS of PEACE   REPLANTED PAPER

Insight Editions, in association with Roots of Peace, will plant
two trees for each tree used in the manufacturing of this book.
Roots of Peace is an internationally renowned humanitarian
organization dedicated to eradicating land mines worldwide
and converting war-torn lands into productive farms and wild-
life habitats. Roots of Peace will plant two million fruit and
nut trees in Afghanistan and provide farmers there with the
skills and support necessary for sustainable land use.

Manufactured in China by Insight Editions

10 9 8 7 6 5 4 3 2

About the Author:

Victoria Rosenthal launched her blog, *Pixelated Provisions*,
in 2012 to combine her lifelong passions for video games
and food by recreating consumables found in many of her
favorite games. When she isn't experimenting in the kitchen
and dreaming up new recipes, she spends her days developing
graphics for NASA. She resides in Houston, Texas, with her
husband and corgi. Victoria is also the author of *Fallout: The
Vault Dweller's Official Cookbook*.

Acknowledgments:

Thanks to Jeff Rosenthal, Harry Readinger, Brandon
Quiocho, Rene Rodriguez, Phil Tibitoski, Carlos Rodriguez,
Nick Esparza, Chris Lytle, Kanji, Kate McKean, Traci Knight,
Michele Rosenthal, Richard Poskozim, Kevin Stich, and my
family for supporting my endeavors during this book.

Insight Editions would like to thank Eric Newgard of
Aurum Effects.

Insight Editions would also like to thank a few individuals
at Bungie that directly helped in the process of creating
this book—Devon Detbrenner, Christine Feraday, Chris
Hausermann, Tim Hernandez, Stacey Janssen, Katie Lennox,
Lorraine McLees, Garrett Morlan, Kevin O'Hara, and
Christine Thompson.